The Ministry of Music in the Church

The Ministry of Music in the Church

Vic Delamont

B.R.E., B.S.M., M.Sc., D.Min. (Cand.)

MOODY PRESS

CHICAGO

Library of Congress Cataloging in Publication Data

Delamont, Vic.
The ministry of music in the church.

Bibliography: p.
Includes index.
1. Church music—Protestant churches. 2. Church music—North America. I. Title.
ML3110.D44 783'.026 79-25918
ISBN 0-8024-5673-1

3 4 5 6 7 Printing/LC/Year 87 86 85 84 83

Printed in the United States of America

Dedicated with love to Bev

O sing unto the LORD a new song;
sing unto the LORD, all the earth.

Sing unto the LORD, bless his name;
shew forth his salvation from day to day.

Declare his glory among the heathen,
his wonders among all people.

For the LORD is great, and greatly to be praised:
he is to be feared above all gods.

For all the gods of the nations are idols:
but the LORD made the heavens.

Honour and majesty are before him:
strength and beauty are in his sanctuary.

Give unto the LORD, O ye kindreds of the people,
give unto the LORD glory and strength.

Give unto the LORD the glory due unto his name:
bring an offering, and come into his courts.

O worship the LORD in the beauty of holiness:
fear before him, all the earth.

Say among the heathen that the LORD reigneth:
the world also shall be established that it
shall not be moved:
he shall judge the people righteously.

Let the heavens rejoice, and let the earth
be glad;
let the sea roar, and the fulness thereof.

Let the field be joyful, and all that is therein:
then shall all the trees of the wood rejoice

Before the LORD: for he cometh,
for he cometh to judge the earth:
he shall judge the world with righteousness,
and the people with his truth.

PSALM 96

Contents

Introduction

The purpose of this book is to provide a practical guide for the music ministry of the local church. In it is information to assist all the leaders of the church in their dealings with the music of the church. My intention was to provide a book for the needs of that select yet multitudinous group of churches and peoples known as the typical North American evangelical church, be it Baptist, Alliance, Evangelical Free, Nazarene, or other. The scope of this book is large enough to encompass the needs of the large church, but it contains hints for enhancing the ministry of music in the small church as well. The book suggests what leadership positions there should be in a music program, the requirements for those leadership positions, and ideas that may help the leaders do their jobs better.

My sincere desire is that this work will make someone's task easier and his ministry more effective. I wrote this handbook for lay leaders, beginning professional musicians in the church, pastors, board members, and committee members across the land who need some simple, straightforward, rubber-meets-the-road information on how to establish and maintain a significant *ministry* through the medium of music.

1

Developing a Philosophy of Music Ministry

Why Have Music in the Church?

Without doubt, the most significant decision to be made by anyone involved in a church's music ministry is the decision concerning a philosophy of music ministry. It is not sufficient for a person to know how to get people in a church to produce music, nor is it sufficient for him to know what to do when and where; behind those abilities must be a solid, carefully thought out answer to this question: Why should there be music in church?

Commands

A first answer to that question is that God commands that music be used in the church. Most Christians are familiar with the Old Testament commands to praise God with singing and instruments, particularly those commands found in the Psalms, the hymnbook of ancient Israel. Psalm 81 and others do not present alternatives; rather they dictate that we are to "Sing aloud unto God our strength: make a joyful noise unto the God of Jacob" (Psalm 81:1). Music was to be used to express delight in the Lord, to communicate that delight to others, and to offer praise and worship to God. As with most prayers recorded in Scripture, most songs are praise (e.g., Psalms 47 and 96), though many are also designed as teaching tools (e.g., Phil. 2:5-11, an early Christian hymn; see also Col.

3:16) and others are given as evangelistic admonitions (see Pslam 108:1-3; Isa. 42:10-12). Indeed, many pages could be filled with biblical admonitions to make music and with examples of biblical songs. I believe that God commands the use of music in the three areas just referred to: in worship, or praise; in teaching, or discipleship; and in outreach, or evangelism.

Traditions

A second reason for having music in the church is the tradition of using music in worship, a tradition that has been firmly established from the use of the Levitical choirs (1 Chron. 15:16; 2 Chron. 29:25-28) to the New Testament practice of "making melody in your heart to the Lord" (Eph. 5:19; see also Luke 1:26-38, 46-55, 68-79; 2:10-14, 29-35; Acts 16:25; James 5:13). This tradition was continued by the early church, added to by the Reformers, continues on to this day (though briefly interrupted by papal bulls and changing traditions), and will continue throughout eternity (Rev. 14:2-3; 15:2-3).

The Psalms were the fare of Calvin and the Reformed tradition, while Luther preferred hymns and was very favorable to music in the church. Watts and Wesley, who followed later, introduced the gospel songs. These three kinds of church music had different emphases and uses, but most of them emphasized the biblical themes of joy and gladness, praise and adoration. It is also interesting that the Psalms are primarily worship (praise), the hymns largely speak of the Christian life, and the gospel songs address themselves to testimony and outreach. Surely the traditions of earlier Christians, along with the promise of song through eternity, are valuable guides in determining the reason for music in the church today.

Intrinsic value

A third reason for having music in the church is that the medium itself, through the ministry of the Holy Spirit, has the intrinsic ability to lead people in worship, to attract people to Christ, and to serve admirably as a vehicle for learning about the Christian life. Music in and of itself can communicate (see chapter five), yet music in and of itself is not always the best method of communication. Communication in worship must be accurate—"in spirit and in truth" (John 4:23-24); it must be coupled with solid knowledge—"I will sing with the understanding also" (1 Cor. 14:15); and, finally, it must lead men to God for His glory (Psalm 107:8; Rom. 10:13-17). The ultimate purpose of man is the glory of God; therefore, the glory of God must be the basis of the philosophy of ministry in music or anything else. Music must not degenerate into a manipulating device—that is, a tool to achieve other ends—by the control of people's emotions, for instance.

The Purpose of Music in the Church

Any ministry that hopes for a lasting effect must incorporate into its program three earlier-mentioned activities—worship, evangelism, and discipleship. Any individual, committee, board, or church that majors on one of those activities to the exclusion of the other two will ultimately change to absorb all three, or will fail. A balanced, growing, and vitally functioning Christian ministry must support all three of those activities.

Simply defined, *worship* is giving to God the glory, praise, honor, and thanks due Him, both for who He is and for what He has done. *Evangelism* is any aspect of ministry that is concerned with the ultimate end of drawing individuals to a personal, saving knowledge of Jesus Christ by grace through faith in His shed blood alone to pay for their sins. *Discipleship* is taking those individuals from their recognition of that saving knowledge to a position of spiritual maturity, which comes via heavy exposure to the Word of God, practical Christian living in light of the Word of God, and a concern for others. Discipleship includes understanding the messages of the songs sung, and it also includes the training of new musicians, directors, accompanists, librarians, and others for work within the church. These three elements feed each other and thus are self-perpetuating. Taken together, they constitute the purpose of church music.

Spiritual Gifts; Abilities and Talents; Christian Responsibility; and Music Ministry

A consideration of spiritual gifts, abilities and talents, and Christian responsibility also figures significantly in a biblical philosophy of music.

Spiritual gifts

Every Christian is endowed by the Holy Spirit with a special gift, or with special gifts, which are supernatural abilities for the express purpose of building up the body of Christ. These gifts are outlined in Romans 12:6-8; 1 Corinthians 12:8-10, 28-30; Ephesians 4:11; and other related passages. Music is not listed as a spiritual gift in any of those references; yet much emphasis is placed on it. Can that emphasis be justified? I believe so. Speech is not a spiritual gift; yet preaching, prophecy, and exhortation all rely on it as a vehicle for communication of the message. Music as well is a vehicle for communication of gifts. Thus both speech and music, which are not listed as gifts of the Spirit, are media through which gifts of the Spirit can be manifested.

Music may encourage, comfort, challenge, exhort, lead, or stir, but only as it is exercised under the guidance and power of the Holy Spirit for the glory of God. In other words, just as a person may be a great orator but not have a ministry, so a person can be a great musician and not have a ministry. That seems obvious, and it is; yet the ramifications may not be. A large portion of this book deals with ministry and the qualifications of those who minister, but persons without the indwelling Holy Spirit (that is, unregenerate persons) *cannot* minister to the church, because they cannot be the recipients of spiritual gifts. For without an attitude that is controlled by God, no *ministering* will be done on a regular basis. Music may be performed; but lives will not be changed, needs will not be met, and God will not be glorified. Only the members of the body of Christ are used to minister the life of Christ on a regular basis. This is not to say that God cannot and does not use circumstances and non-Christians as He will, but it is to say that those situations are not a source of ministry as it is outlined in the New Testament.

Two kinds of recognition are called for in the area of spiritual gifts: (1) We must recognize gifts in ourselves, and (2) we must recognize them in others. Each Christian should strive to discover his own spritual gift, but, more important, he should also see and acknowledge the spiritual gifts of other individuals. Many books have been written on discovering one's spiritual gift, so time will not be taken here to discuss it beyond this: Each Christian should ask himself: Does it appear that God is using me for His glory when I do this thing; are people touched by God and drawn to Him? The second point, that of recognizing gifts in others, is not spoken of quite so commonly. I am convinced that if more Christians were looking for the gifts of others, far more would be happening in the church of Christ. Moreover, if people were simply told that others feel that they do, or do not, have a gift in a given area, much frustration would pass away for all concerned.

Abilities, talents, and Christian responsibility

While spiritual gifts are supernatural enablements to do a work within the body of Christ, abilities and talents are natural endowments. They may serve either as media for spiritual gifts (as has already been mentioned) or as acts of Christian responsibility.

The responsibility of a Christian who has a talent or ability is that he use that talent or ability to the glory of God. For instance, although some Christians have the gift of evangelism, all Christians are responsible for being witnesses to the best of their ability. Again—although some have the gift of administration, all are expected to be the best stewards they can with the resources entrusted to them. And although some have a gifted evangelistic or prophetic ministry in song, all are responsible for using the musical abilities they have; for *all* are commanded to praise the Lord in song, no matter how little musical ability they have. I am not proposing that each individual in a congregation is capable of singing a solo on Sunday morning. What I am proposing is that those who are capable of singing solos are expected, as good stewards of their talent, to do so.

(It is likely that many choir members will be *gifted* teachers, evangelists, helpers, or administrators as well as *talented* Christians who are committed to Christ to the extent of wanting to utilize all of their beings to His glory and who are not content to work only in the areas for which they are supernaturally gifted.)

Developing a Philosophy of Music Ministry

Objectives and goals

"Success is getting where you want to go.
Failure is stopping before you get there."[1]

This simple quotation assumes, tacitly, many things. The first thing in "getting there" is to have a "there." Every person who wants to develop a philosophy of music ministry should ask himself these questions: What are my goals? What are my objectives? What are my expectations of myself, the program, and other people?

Objectives are commonly thought of as statements of intentions to act, but they do not include any element of time. *Goals* are statements of intentions to achieve results of measurable quality and quantity by a certain time. By this definition, then, having goals thus includes having two things:

(1) written (or at least accurately thought out) objectives—but with timetables and expected results added, and

---

[1]Paul B. Welleford, "Tragedy to Triumph," *The Church Musician* 25, no. 1 (October 1973):13. From *The Church Musician*, Oct. 1973. © Copyright The Sunday School Board of the Southern Baptist Convention. All rights reserved. Used by permission.

(2) a method of measurement or evaluation to see if the results indicate whether or not the goals have been realized.

By way of illustration, a leader's objective may be to have as many people as possible involved in the music ministry of his church. He then sets the specific goal of rehearsing a fourteen-member men's chorus by October 1. Evaluation is simple: Did the group start rehearsing by October 1, and did it have a membership of fourteen? Goals like "assure good choral diction by the end of June" are more difficult to evaluate because of the subjective nature of evaluating "good." Such a goal should be broken down into several goals with specific levels of achievement for different parts of good diction—for example, "unity of word endings with only three errors per number by the end of April." Achievement of the initial goal ("good diction by the end of June") comes when the constituent goals have all been achieved.

Objectives

Objectives for a music ministry might include such things as:

1. Developing a philosophy of ministry
2. Developing directors, soloists, accompanists, and choir-section leaders
3. Increasing enrollment
4. Forming clear statements of doctrine, biblical truths, denominational distinctives, and music appreciation
5. Improving sight-reading, diction, knowledge of theory, voice production, and so forth in the various choirs
6. Improving one's own knowledge of conducting and one's skill in conducting and playing

Though there are many more, some other objectives for a music ministry are:

7. Achieving one's own expectations for his music program and personnel, as well as achieving the expectations of the music committee and those of the congregation, board, or

senior pastor (ideally these expectations would all be the same)

8. Achieving outreach, discipleship, and worship
9. Defining responsibilities for all positions
10. Coordinating all church activities
11. Implementing family ministries (or other specialized ministries)
12. Recruiting personnel
13. Developing personnel
14. Training accompanists
15. Developing a repertoire
16. Expanding the music library
17. Improving rehearsal procedures
18. Developing a varied and exciting program
19. Ensuring that the attitude of all participants is that of wanting to have a significant ministry
20. Establishing personal and professional priorities

The above examples give an idea of the kinds of things to be considered in setting objectives. Each of them could be expanded and added to. Consider number twenty, for instance. Priorities could be listed in areas of philosophy, practice, performance, recruitment, personnel, groups, and so on. The order of priorities for groups, for example, might look like this:

1. Leadership generally
2. Senior choir
3. Congregational singing
4. Other choirs
   - A. Youth
   - B. Chancel (small group, best singers)
   - C. Junior
   - D. Ladies'
   - E. Men's
   - F. Clubs'
   - G. Senior citizens'

H. Primary
5. Sunday school music
6. Equipment
7. Training individuals
   A. Song leaders
   B. Directors
   C. Accompanists
   D. Music committee personnel
   E. Section leaders
   F. Librarians
8. Instrumental music
   A. Accompaniment of groups or soloists
   B. Orchestra
   C. Ensemble
   D. Band
   E. Soloists

This is, in part, the kind of detailed work that permits a church, board, committee, or individual working as director or minister of music to see exactly what is involved and what plan of attack to use in the various parts of a certain area. It is obviously time consuming, but it pays off in organization, in unity of aim, and, when one looks back and evaluates his progress, in the confidence that things *are* happening.

Goals

Setting goals involves breaking generalized objectives down into specific objectives that are to be achieved by a certain time. It is good to commit goals to writing. The methods put into use to realize goals are often called tactics. They should also be written down.

Evaluation

Evaluation is important to more people than just the leaders. People will commit themselves only to that which they feel is worthwhile. Evaluation will point out to the leaders and to the members that what is being done either is or is not worth their time and effort.

One important point in evaluation is this: If a program or activity is not serving its designed purpose, it should be changed or thrown out. No one is perfect, and no one needs to be afraid to admit to an error of judgment. People involved in the music ministry should be concerned about meeting needs and serving in their ministry, but they should not be concerned with keeping their pet programs running regardless of their usefulness, their benefits, or the attitudes behind them. Yet this pragmatic approach must be tempered with an appreciation of the specific goal of the program or activity in question. This is where clearly defined goals can help. If the goal for a particular number is merely to make the congregation feel warmed, and if the song does that, the goal has been achieved.

Evaluation is based on measurement of definables. Part of the reason for establishing goals and objectives, as well as the tactics that will be implemented to achieve them, is to ensure unity within the group, though not at the price of sacrificing basic doctrine for it. Unification of purpose and philosophy is mandatory for everyone involved in the music ministry. Variations of personal tastes and preferences can be worked out, but the basic tenets of ministry must be agreed upon by all involved. Further, these basic matters should be discussed, evaluated, and openly considered to ensure that the basic premises of the church are accurate, understood, and built upon in practice.

A Practical Illustration

Consider, as a point of illustration, the use of non-Christians in the music program, as referred to earlier. Three camps emerge on this question: (1) those who feel that this is an invaluable tool of outreach, particularly among youth, (2) those who feel that ministry cannot take place through an unregenerate person, and (3) those who cannot decide and those who refuse to grapple with the problem. Looking at the ramifications of this question will give practice at making the decisions necessary for arriving at a sound philosophy of ministry.

Often a chartlike arrangement is helpful in comparing views in this kind of situation. But before a chart is constructed, the third position, which is untenable, must be ruled out: The question must be faced and dealt with, and a decision must be made. Therefore, only views one and two need be charted.

QUESTION: Should non-Christians be used in the music program of the church?

VIEWS:	YES	NO
REASONS:	provides a good environment for non-Christians; allows them to be with Christians	(agree)
	gives an opportunity for witness by the Christian members of the group and their leaders	(agree)
	helps provide a maximum exposure to Christianity so that evidences of believing will or will not appear in the persons in question	(agree)
	does not exclude any of the church family, particularly young children of members and so forth	(agree)

VIEWS:	YES	NO
REASONS:	(disagree; they sing as part of the group, which ministers)	expects a spiritual ministry from those who are spiritually dead
	(that need not happen here)	"bad apple" theory
	(agree, but . . .)	expects unregenerate persons, who are not members of the body of Christ, to perform the Christian responsibility of caring for members of the body, a responsibility for which they are not fit
	(agree)	may lead persons functioning as Christians to a false security that they indeed are Christians, because they live and do what others (Christians) apparently do
	as long as they are committed to the program (or living moral lives, etc.), non-Christians are less trouble than Christians who are acting carnally	(possibly, but commitment to the program is nothing: commitment to Christ is everything)

VIEWS:	YES	NO
REASONS:	there are more of "them" than there are of "us"; and many of them are better musicians whose talents we need	(but what does God desire except our loving response to Him as Savior and Lord? God is not impressed with the talents of men)
	exception: do not let non-Christians preach, witness, or sing solos	(what is the difference? The non-Christians will still be involved in parts of the ministry of the Christian life)
	(what is the difference?)	exception: young children should be encouraged and allowed to join children's choirs; non-Christians will, for the most part, drop out by junior high age; only professing Christians should be admitted to groups beyond junior high.
	(agree)	exception: if the group members (including non-Christians) have the repertoire, let them hold a concert; but bill it as such, not as a service

Obviously more could be said on both sides, but these are the arguments that usually come up. Now—how is the decision made? Is it based on the number of positive points each side has, the side with more positive points winning? Or is it based on the relative weight of the arguments? Both are to be considered. My conclusion is that non-Christians ought not to be included in the ministry, and that conclusion can stand reasonably firmly on the single tenet that non-Christians have nothing to minister.

The importance of organization, planning, preparation, and clear headed determination cannot be underestimated. Whether one is pastor, director, board member, or choir member, he is affected by just such matters as that of the place of non-Christians in the choir. If ministry is to occur, it must be prepared for in every possible way to ensure its success. If leaders are to lead others, they must be prepared, organized, and determined, and they must have a plan. Obviously, leadership carries weights of responsibility that must not be taken lightly or for granted. It is imperative that all who function as church leaders, in any field, have a biblically based and well defined philosophy of ministry before moving on to create the resultant atmosphere of the church.

2

Qualifications of Personnel in the Music Program

In this chapter we shall consider the ideal qualifications for the minister of music, pianists, organists, directors, and music committee members who will guide the church to God through music. It should be kept in mind that persons who meet all these requirements do not in fact exist. Each church must establish its priorities from the lists and seek persons who best fit those priorities.

Minister of Music

There are both personal and functional qualifications that must be considered for anyone applying for any job. For the position of minister of music, the personal qualifications are at least as important as the functional ones, and very probably more important.

Personal qualifications

The personal qualifications of the minister of music include:

1. The recognition that love for God, His Word, and the church is as important as a love for music
2. A sense of mission—wanting to reach and develop people for Christ, recognizing the minister of music's place in realizing that objective, and having abilities to fulfill it
3. A personal philosophy based on the Word of God and compatible with the other pastors and that church with which he will work

4. A knowledge of denominational distinctives and agreement with them
5. Complete dedication to Christ, His church, and the tasks of the minister of music
6. Good physical condition and an energetic attitude
7. Organizational and administrative abilities, and the ability to delegate responsibility and supervise without interfering; Austin Lovelace and William Rice suggest that "the efficient director will accept the fact that he cannot do everything"[1]; I suggest that he *must* not do everything
8. A cooperative attitude toward others
9. A sensitivity to the needs of individuals and to the needs of the church as a whole
10. The talent of getting to know a choir as individuals
11. Confidence
12. Courage
13. Dependability, punctuality, and personal discipline
14. The ability to evaluate himself and others, then make a decision and act accordingly
15. Emotional stability
16. Social maturity
17. Enthusiasm tempered with common sense (which, incidentally is not so common)
18. Neatness of person
19. Poise and tact
20. A sense of humor
21. An attractive personality—that is, a bit of sparkle (this trait is often labeled as unnecessary in the Lord's work, but in fact it is required, albeit tacitly, by the congregation)
22. A bent towards both professional and personal growth in his ministry and in his life
23. The ability to understand and empathize with others—a gracious attitude

[1]Austin C Lovelace and William C. Rice, *Music and Worship in the Church* (Nashville: Abingdon, 1976), p. 66.

24. The ability and willingness to work hard
25. The ability to be a self-starter
26. A clean personal life-style
27. Patience
28. More patience
29. An openness to new ideas and music (DeVinney says that "if you do not remain open to new ideas and different kinds of music, your congregation will very quickly cease to listen to you; they already know what you will say"[2])
30. Lovelace and Rice sum up the qualifications beautifully in this paragraph:

> The successful church musician is that fairly rare individual who has somehow maintained good contact with people and with God while promoting his musical growth. He has temperament without being temperamental. In brief, he is a sincere Christian, completely dedicated to his work, for which he is qualified by reason of his native talent and training. He is an excellent musician, but, even more important, he is a person of character who recognizes that his own personal development will affect the expansion of his church and its music program. He has accepted in all humility a great and challenging opportunity to serve God and man.[3]

FUNCTIONAL QUALIFICATIONS

The functional qualifications of a minister of music include:

1. Musical expertise in a field useful to the church music program—for example, conducting, keyboard, and vocal skills, with some orchestral or instrumental background
2. Experience at doing the job on some level, for some minimal period of time (though everyone has to have a first job)
3. Some competence as a music historian

[2]Richard DeVinney, *There's More to Church Music Than Meets the Ear* (Philadelphia: Fortress, 1972), p. 54. Copyright © by Fortress Press. Reprinted by permission of Fortress Press.
[3]Lovelace and Rice, p. 68.

4. Training in Christian education, theology, and administration as well as in music
5. The ability to coach voices, individually and in a choir setting (including an ear for balance, vocal technique, and so on)
6. Conducting skills
7. The talents of arranging, orchestrating, and composition
8. A knowledge of instrument maintenance and repair
9. The ability to plan, direct, and evaluate a total music program, including a knowledge of what to include in it
10. Training in staging and drama production
11. Knowledge of building acoustics
12. Some understanding of electronic sound systems
13. A sensitivity to good poetry, and to good hymn and anthem texts
14. Talents and abilities above the average of others in the church
15. The gift of ministry, in order that he might fulfill first the role of minister and second that of musician

Accompanists—Pianists and Organists

Many of the qualifications for different positions in the church are the same, but here is a listing of those which should be considered valuable for pianists and organists. Many of these qualifications could apply to the minister of music, and many of his qualifications could apply here:

1. Christian training both in theology and in church music
2. Dedication to Christ and His church
3. Stamina
4. Sincerity
5. Poise
6. Humility
7. Dependability
8. Self-confidence
9. Emotional and social maturity
10. Tact

11. A sense of humor
12. An attitude of cooperation toward others
13. The ability to accept suggestions and criticism
14. Punctuality
15. The ability to think and react quickly in unexpected situations, and to recover well
16. A spouse who is positive to the accompanist's heavy involvement in the music program, allowing time for practice, rehearsals, regular services, and so forth
17. Good taste in apparel and in music
18. A sense of artistry that is able to interpret music and make it live, not a "mechanic" who gets it "book right" without sensitivity
19. A desire to improve
20. A willingness and ability to teach his skills to others
21. A knowledge of the instrument played
22. Patience
23. The ability to *accompany*, without rushing ahead or dragging behind
24. The ability to work under a conductor
25. Flexibility
26. The ability to sight-read
27. The ability to improvise and play by ear
28. The ability to transpose (this includes a knowledge of modulation from key to key)
29. A good solo repertoire
30. Enjoyment of playing
31. Some vocal training
32. A desire to serve in this demanding capacity and to be auditioned carefully before serving

Directors—Vocal and Instrumental

The director of any musical group should possess the same general characteristics as those for ministers of music and accompanists, plus the following:

1. The ability to read the score of whatever group he is

directing with enough accuracy to *lead* each section and not simply follow what it is doing

2. Sufficient musical knowledge and personal expertise to give direction, sing a part, demonstrate a rhythm, define a term, or perform any other of the usual assortment of musical duties

3. A determination to lead, develop, and guide the group to higher musical and personal standards; and the necessary gifts, abilities, and talents to do so

4. The ability to communicate both specific and abstract concepts to the group

5. Training in conducting, theory, musical style, form, and theology, so that the music he selects will be of good musical and doctrinal quality, and be aesthetically pleasing

6. An openness to the guidance, criticism, and suggestions of the minister of music and the music committee, and the maturity to accept, evaluate, and respond to their comments with appropriate attitudes and action

7. All the expected characteristics of punctuality, deportment, self-discipline, and so on already spoken of in other contexts

Music Committee Members

Like the others, this list is not exhaustive: it is given in addition to those qualifications already mentioned. It is not required that each member of the committee have the suggested qualifications, but it is important that the committee as a group have them:

1. The gift of administration
2. An understanding of the music available for use in the church
3. A sensitivity to the needs and preferences of the congregation
4. Some awareness of the capabilities of the various musical groups and individual musicians in order to evaluate them, decide on special music for the services, and so forth

5. Familiarity with the job description of each person in the music department, in order to evaluate his performance accurately
6. At least one member with a good ear, so that he can sit in various locations in the services and listen for people in the congregation who sing well; those people may later be approached about serving in music in some way
7. The skills necessary to promote the music department of the church at all levels—administrative and public
8. The willingness and ability to make a decision that may involve removing someone from participation in the music program, should there be sufficient reason
9. The desire to support the ministry of music in all its parts
10. Artistry, imagination, and creativity, which may be employed not only to guide the music program but also to advise any efforts in drama or other forms of the arts within the church

3

Organization and Administration of the Music Program

Organization of the Local Church

The biblical organizational structure of the church is to be viewed with two ideas in mind. One of those ideas is that all believers are equal in status before God; and that idea is true. The other idea is that God has ordained lines of authority; and that idea is also true. Most North American evangelical churches are structured somewhat in line with the chart below. (Please note that because the congregation's position will vary depending on the type of church government, reference to the congregation is omitted for clarity.) The ensuing job descriptions are only suggestions and will need to be altered to fit the character of the individual church as it sees fit, but they are broad enough to fit most situations. (Next page.)

The pastors are the shepherds who are "doubly responsible" for the care of the flock. Elders or deacons watch over the congregation with gentle, knowing precision. The various committees that may be formed under the direction of the leaders carry out their leadership and maintain the efficient functioning of the local body of believers. There may be various subcommittees, such as a platform committee, an audiovisual committee, a visitation committee, and so forth, depending on the size and program of the individual church. The next several pages cover some sample job descriptions for each of those

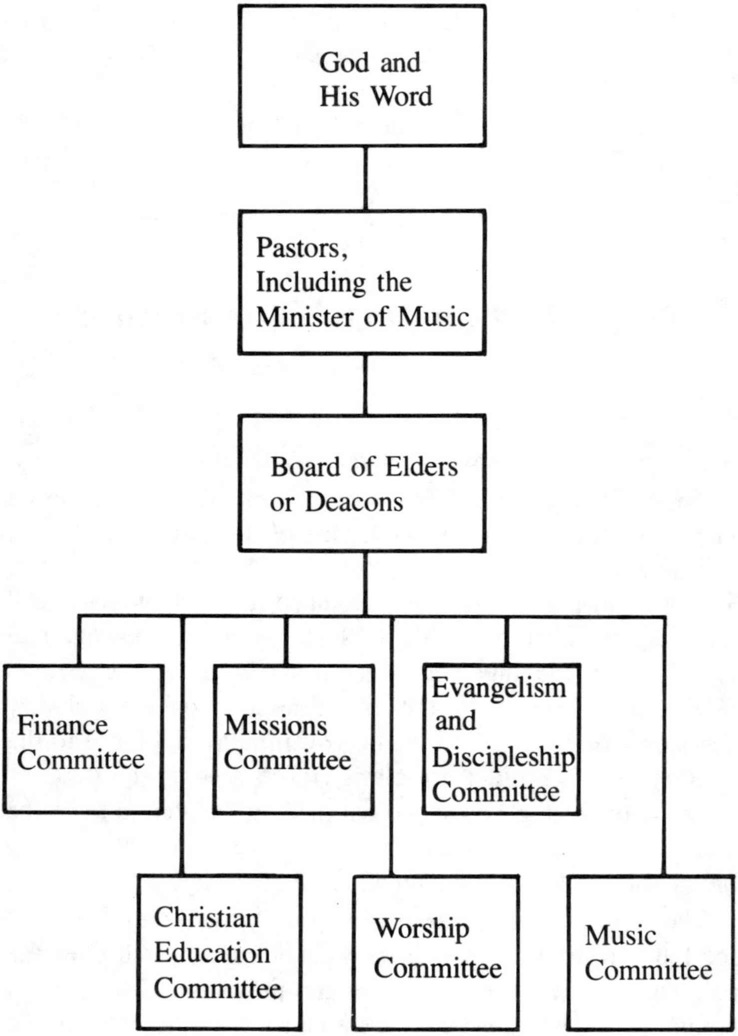

persons involved with the music program. (It should be noted that only the qualifications that relate either directly or indirectly to the music program are given here.) Following the job descriptions are comments on interpersonal relationships in the music program.

One of the most important things to remember about a job description is that it should be in writing before anyone starts performing the job in question. When someone is already serving, that procedure is impossible. But when a new person is starting in a position, he should have the job description before he begins. Further, the content of any job description must be custom tailored to the individual church and to the person or persons involved. It is pointless to insist on the role of organist/choir director, for example, from a person who is superior as a conductor but incompetent as an organist. I hope that these pages will serve as a guide for and a stimulus to careful consideration of the tasks to be performed by each person involved in the administration of the music ministry so that both he and the church are aware of the responsibilities involved.

Senior Minister

The ultimate responsibility for the total church program rests on the senior minister. He must be aware of every function within the church program, and he must be in control of the entire program. However, he must not feel as if he needs to be in *actual* control of each function. Administrative responsibility must not be fatally confused with the insecure need actually to do everything in the church or to be involved in every facet of its ministry. The pastoral staff, as leaders, must lead, initiate, and support. In a very small church as well as in a very large one, the senior minister should make every reasonable attempt to be aware of the significance of music in his church. Further, he should, in conference with the minister of music or the song leader, help select the hymns for the services to the extent that he feels capable, or to the extent that his involvement is desirable or necessary. Moreover, he should seek to communicate to persons in the music department, individually or in groups:

1. His appreciation of their work and ministry
2. His aims and aspirations for the church's future and their

parts in the realization of those aims and aspirations

3. His willingness to receive their comments regarding the music department in particular

4. The philosophy of ministry he espouses and feels should be that of the ministry of all areas of the church

Minister of Music

The Minister of Music is the chief executive of the music program, under the headship of the senior minister. He should not be responsible to any board or committee, but to the senior minister alone. (This system avoids a plurality of bosses, loyalties, or philosophies.) The minister of music makes all final decisions regarding the music program, and other persons in the music program should be made aware of his authority in that area. He is in charge of the entire church music program, and he must be able to handle that responsibility.

1. His first priority is the choir program, beginning with the senior choir and adding others as personnel, finances, and scheduling will permit, until a fully integrated, graded choir program is usefully functioning.
2. He is intimately involved with all long-range planning, not just with planning that pertains to music (with an aim to unity).
3. He serves as a music teacher, preparing conductors, arrangers, composers, accompanists, and performers as much as he can.
4. He delegates as much responsibility as he deems reasonable to other persons in the music department.
5. He serves as conductor of the senior choir and, at his discretion, of other groups; he advises and assists, where necessary, those groups he does not direct.
6. He arranges or composes music primarily for the use of the church, although such works may be released for publication without further commitment to the church.
7. He plans thoroughly all the musical activities of the church so that things may be acceptable and in good order to

the glory of God and the trust of his fellow believers.

8. He seeks professional growth through:
   A. Taking time to read, study, and practice in his performance medium
   B. Meeting other musicians to discuss ideas
   C. Continuing his study of Scripture and theology in a constant effort to live a Spirit-filled life
   D. Accurately assessing his own strengths and weaknesses, and acting accordingly
   E. Attending all regular church services
   F. Taking advantage of local workshops and opportunities for further study, and once or twice a year attending a major conference that is agreeable to himself, the church, and the senior minister

9. He welcomes chances to work with other departments of the church, particularly the worship and Christian education departments, thus striving to make music an integrated part of all church life.

10. He has a personal ministry in keeping with his gifts, talents, and abilities.

11. He seeks to fit his music to the needs of the people in the congregation, not trying to force upon them his favorite style, yet striving to expand their horizons of appreciation and honor God in all, thus developing both the music and the music library; this is well done in cooperation with the organist, the pianist, and others in the program.

12. He is an active listener to:
   A. The music of the church
   B. The views of members of the church
   C. Recitals, concerts, operas, tapes, records, and such expressions as may increase his value and strengthen his service to God and his church

13. He is responsible for instrument maintenance and repair, the purchase and cataloging of music, and other budget expenditures, in coordination with the finance and music committees and the other pastoral staff.

14. He keeps accurate records and files of:
    A. Expenditures (music purchases, for example, could be listed by title, date, cost per copy, number of copies, total cost, and balance remaining)
    B. Music used by title, date, and book
    C. Hymns used by title and date
    D. Special music (persons and selections) used by name, title, and date
15. He is ex officio on the church board, the music committee, the worship committee, the audiovisual committee, the Christian education committee, and the platform committee.
16. He is responsible for the organization and administration of the entire music program, including:
    A. Establishing objectives, goals, and tactics
    B. Leading in Christian and musical growth: endeavoring to stimulate a positive response to God through music and through his personal life
    C. Comforting, encouraging, strengthening, and training people in his care
    D. Delegating responsibility
    E. Caring for the buildings and equipment necessary for the efficient functioning of the music program
    F. Ensuring that the music committee is aware of its responsibilities
    G. Establishing a policy for lending and borrowing music
    H. Advising the church board as to exactly how much a good music program will cost in finances, resources, personnel, and time
    I. Developing the special music personnel and regular program personnel both quantitatively and qualitatively
17. He should be aware of the totality of the musical world and its changes; he should be somewhat involved in secular musical life, such as national music organizations, so that he might learn from others and be a witness for Christ to those who might not otherwise have a witness; membership in

professional organizations will also provide fresh ideas and techniques.

18. He constantly evaluates the music program.

19. In consideration of the above-mentioned duties, he is paid in relation to services offered, education, and experience, on an approximate par with others doing similar work (that is, other staff members, teachers, or musicians), as much as the church is able.

20. His appointment is permanent.

Choir Directors

Senior choir director

1. The senior choir director is responsible for the selection, purchase, rehearsal, and performance of the senior choir's music, which will consist of one or two anthems each Sunday morning (plus calls to worship, prayer responses, and so forth as the church is accustomed to or as he should choose).
2. He is responsible for selecting purchasing, rehearsing, and performing such other music as may be desirable—for example, special programs or cantatas at Christmas, Easter, and other times.
3. He strives for excellence of diction, production, tone, understanding, interpretation, and other technicalities of the music from the choir.
4. He recruits members for the choir.
5. He keeps accurate records of each member's name, address, phone numbers (home and work), hobbies, and so forth, along with each member's attendance, part sung, audition, instruments played, other jobs in the church, and so forth.
6. He is responsible for the senior choir library (music stamped with church stamp, filed, and carded), supplies, and vestments.
7. He is able to articulate his objectives and goals based on a minimum one-year plan of future goals and activities.

8. He provides spiritual and musical leadership for the senior choir.

9. He provides for times of fellowship and recreation for the senior choir.

10. He may delegate 4, 5, and 9 above.

11. It is suggested that he also work with and through the formal leader of the choir (the choir executive) and through the informal leaders of the choir to build a group consciousness, not a "me-thee" relationship, in order to achieve, as much as possible, a fellowship and unity of purpose in ministry.

12. He seeks membership in such professional organizations as may be to his benefit (for example, Chorister's Guild, Fellowship of Christian Musicians, Lutheran Committee on Worship and Arts, Gospel Music Association, Music Educators National Conference).

13. His appointment is for one year, with inclusive dates given.

OTHER CHOIR DIRECTORS

Youth, junior, primary, beginners', men's, ladies', Sunday school, club, senior citizens', and other choirs will have directors who function in much the same way as the senior choir director, with variation according to the particular needs and aims of each group. Directors and accompanists should be men for the men's choir, if possible, and ladies for the ladies' choir.

SONG LEADERS

Song leaders lead group singing at the request of the minister of music or the senior minister.

1. Song leaders select hymns ahead of time for the service in which they are to be used (unless hymns are selected by someone else) and go over them with the pianists and or-

ganists who will be accompanying (to establish tempo and so forth).

2. They strive to make the musical experience meaningful, significant, and enjoyable.

3. They use simple conducting, are sure of what they are doing, and are poised, as good representatives of God and the church.

4. They seek assistance from the minister of music (or from someone else should there be no minister of music) as required in order to lead this portion of the worship experience smoothly and accurately[1].

5. Each song leader's appointment is for one year, with inclusive dates given.

Accompanists—Pianists and Organists

1. Accompanists (pianists and organists) make every necessary effort to maintain and improve their performance skills, their ability to *accompany* (not follow or lead)[2] those with whom they are ministering, and their sensitivity both in their musical styles and in their Christian lives.

2. They practice as required to play at the best of their abilities (the church instruments may be scheduled for their practice times).

3. They attend all regular and special services and rehearsals in which they are to participate, with the understanding that all special items will be cleared with them ahead of time.

4. They know the contents of chapter 5, "Determining Appropriateness," and try to select their material accordingly.

5. They endeavor to teach (disciple) others in the skills of hymn playing, accompaniment, solo work, and improvisation, and in the personal attitudes that enhance their

---

[1] Robert O. Hoffelt's *How to Lead Informal Singing* (Nashville: Abingdon, 1961) is a good resource for beginning directors.

[2] From William S. Mathis, *The Pianist and Church Music* (Nashville: Abingdon, 1962), p. 86.

ministry.

6. They play in the manner, style, tempo, and volume dictated by the director (or, when there is no director, they will play as sensitive taste leads).

7. They assume such particular duties as are demanded by their individual positions, as follows:

   A. The Sunday morning pianist and organist are responsible for accompanying the senior choir

   B. The Sunday evening pianist and organist are responsible for accompanying the youth choir

   C. Sunday school accompanists (any department) are responsible for accompanying any regular Sunday school choirs or groups

   D. All who play preludes begin them ten to fifteen minutes before the service is to begin; preludes are played with an attitude of leading in worship, not used as opportunities for showing skill or as mere preparations for worship

   E. Exceptions to A-D above are permissible with the approval of the music committee in agreement with the minister of music

   F. All accompanists perform such other reasonable duties as may be requested by the music committee or the minister of music

8. They strive to be faithful and responsible in executing their duties.

9. Their appointments are for one year, with inclusive dates given.

PIANISTS

It is sometimes said by pianists and piano salesmen alike that a good piano is worth a dozen bad organs, and that a good pianist is worth a dozen bad organists—try to be that good!

1. The choir pianist should remember that "playing the piano accurately and precisely is meaningless unless the accuracy and precision are used to convey musical mean-

ing''[3]; in all accompaniment, it is important to realize that the pianist's role is of extreme importance; nonmechanical sensitivity to the mood, content, and style of the music must be present in the accompaniment (a firm touch for large group singing and tasteful improvisation for solo accompaniment are examples of such sensitivity).

2. The pianist accompanies the hymns, following the song leader carefully.
3. He alternates offertories with the church organist, at their discretion.
4. He is prepared to participate in concerts or recitals (at the request of the music committee in consultation with the minister of music), if qualified.

ORGANISTS

The organist endeavors to do all that is required by the music committee (as agreed to by the minister of music) and by good taste to enhance the worship of all who attend, taking care not to alienate but to lead and unite.

1. He makes sure that the character of the preludes, offertories, and postludes fits the nature and intention of the church and the particular service: often people are lead to meditate and worship if a familiar hymn or song is used, and in that way the congregation can think on the words they know; in some instances, however, one may want the congregation to think of something other than the hymn being played, and in that case a lesser-known work, like a prelude and fugue, may be more appropriate; appropriateness is the key.
2. He should remember that hymn accompaniment is the most important aspect of the organist's ministry; then comes accompaniment, and then solo work; he endeavors to improve his skills in those areas, and in that order of priority.
3. He attempts to become proficient at making piano accom-

[3]Mathis, p. 35.

paniments (as are found in many choir anthems) into organ accompaniments.

4. He seeks to expand his knowledge of registration, color, and texture in order to get the best out of the available instrument; and he seeks to expand his knowledge of modulation, transposition, and improvisation in order to get the best out of the player.

5. He recognizes that "solos are an offering to God, and not . . . background music to cover up the sound of footsteps, whispering, or the clinking of money"[4]; he keeps in mind, therefore, the importance of his position and ministers accordingly.

6. He is prepared to participate in concerts and recitals (at the request of the music committee in consultation with the minister of music).

7. He accompanies the hymns, following the song leader carefully.

8. He alternates offertories with the church pianist, at their discretion.

Music Committee

The music committee is responsible, under the guidance of the minister of music, for the functioning of the music program. It should be composed of a member of the church board (who will serve as its chairman), a representative from each of the following committees: Christian education, worship, audiovisual, a representative from each of the regular church-sponsored music groups, and two elected members from the congregation. The minister of music, church pianist, church organist, directors, senior minister, and church board chairman are ex officio members.

1. Music committee members should be sensitive to the musical level and tastes of the church and consider them when planning the music they are responsible for; the com-

---

[4]Samuel Walter, *Basic Principles of Service Playing* (Nashville: Abingdon, 1963), p. 25.

mittee members should desire to stretch the musical appreciation of the church, yet they should not cause offense or lethargy in members of the church.

2. Music committee members have a voice in deciding on the church music budget, both as to how much money is required by each group sponsored (for music, vestments, travel expenses, equipment purchases and maintenance, advertising, office supplies, honorariums, and so forth) and as to how the funds are to be spent.

3. They make recommendations as to how many and which music groups should be sponsored by the church.

4. They are responsible for the auditioning and investigation of persons for the positions of church pianists, church organists, directors, and all other personnel who may be required for the church music program.

5. They are responsible for setting the qualifications for directors, accompanists, and those who would minister in solos, duets, and so forth (to present special music), and they are responsible for making recommendations to those persons with the authority to hire a minister of music.

6. They select people to minister who have a personal interest in the music ministry and are capable of getting the job done.

7. Should a person selected for a position not be able to fulfill his commitments through external circumstance or by a lack of personal discipline, ability, or proper attitudes, the members of this committee should take early steps to help the person; if the situation does not improve to a predetermined satisfactory level, they should take prompt action to replace the person, lest the ministry suffer because of a lack of insightful action on their part.

8. They set the policy for the use of church instruments and equipment under their control.

9. They do everything reasonable within their power to assist the minister of music in his every task, striving to achieve the smooth functioning of the program, the efficient use of their

leaders, and the glory of God; they recommend ministry guidelines to the church board, and they recommend leadership guidelines in the music department, then submit to that leadership, as personified in the minister of music, according to Hebrews 13:17, in recognition of his gifts, talents, abilities, education, and position under God.

10. They schedule use of the rehearsal rooms.
11. They are a rotating committee, with members elected for two-year terms, half to be replaced each year; this system helps to ensure a continuity of program and emphasis.

Platform Committee

The platform committee may be either a subcommittee of the worship committee or a distinct committee. The members of the platform committee are responsible for the appearance and equipping of the chancel in preparation for every service.

1. They provide microphones and stands as required for special music, and they make sure that the microphones are on and working, in cooperation with the audio operators.
2. They provide lecterns for performers of special music as required.
3. They provide a lectern for the choir director's music.
4. They ensure sufficient seating, an adequate number of hymnals, and an ample number of copies of the order of service for persons leading the service (including persons performing special music).
5. They provide one glass of iced water per every three persons leading the service; under normal circumstances, most participants will not require the water; even if there are only one or two participants, however, water should always be supplied.
6. They check the arrangement of articles in the chancel area.
7. Before the service begins, they provide, check, and arrange for the operation of any other equipment that may be

required (overhead projector, screen, roving microphone, and so forth).

Worship Committee

The worship committee is responsible for assisting the ministers in supervising all the worship services. One of its members will be a representative on the music committee, where he will carry information back and forth between the two committees in an honest effort at coordinating activities between the two. Because music plays an important part in the worship service, the worship committee will want to coordinate all special services, special requests, and so forth with the music committee.

Audiovisual Committee

Since a great deal of the impact and effectiveness of many of the various music ministries depends on a good, well-operated sound system, the members of the audiovisual committee work closely with the members of the music committee.

1. The members of the audiovisual committee see that the sound-system operators have a reasonable ear for music.
2. These operators should be present at each service at least one-half hour early; in that time they perform the following duties:
   A. They prepare the sound system in cooperation and coordination with the member of the platform committee present; he will have informed them as far in advance as possible of what equipment is required for that particular service.
   B. They preset the volume and filter levels on the equipment for the special music for that particular service.
   C. They check the sound system, prepare for recording the service, and make any other preparations necessary to ensure an interruption-free service in which all may hear without distraction.

Christian Education Committee

1. Members of the Christian education committee cooperate with the minister of music and the music committee in the use of in-training accompanists, soloists, and groups in the Sunday school, clubs, and like groups.
2. They endeavor to provide for classes in music during the Sunday school hour or at such other times as is expedient to the church; classes to consider are:
   A. Conducting and song leading
   B. Hymn playing
   C. Music theory
   D. Class voice lessons
   E. Such others as the music committee or the minister of music recommends

Choir Executives

Each choir from the youth choir up should have a president, a secretary-treasurer, a calling committee chairman, and a social convenor. The responsibilities of each officer are:

President

1. The president communicates, as a liaison between the choir and the director, any "beefs or bouquets," information regarding upcoming events, and so forth.
2. He may serve as assistant choir director, if approved by the music committee.
3. In every way reasonable he assists the choir director in fulfilling his tasks and ministry.

Secretary-treasurer

1. The secretary-treasurer records the attendance of members at each practice and performance; he also passes along to the calling committee chairman the names of any who have missed two consecutive engagements.
2. He takes minutes at executive meetings and has them typed, duplicated, and distributed to the executive as soon as possible after the meeting.

3. He collects the weekly choir dues and keeps accurate records of them; he turns the funds over to the church treasurer, who banks them in the church account; those funds are used for special projects and social events at the simple majority approval of the choir.
4. He is authorized to make expenditures for cards and rose bowls on behalf of the choir for members who are hospitalized, have been bereaved, or have just had a baby.

CALLING COMMITTEE CHAIRMAN

1. The calling committee chairman telephones all members who have been absent from two scheduled choir engagements (names will come from the secretary-treasurer of the choir).
2. He forms a committee to handle mass emergency calling of all members (for example, in the event of a canceled rehearsal or social event); the committee members receive the message from the chairman and quickly pass it on so that no one will be unduly inconvenienced.

SOCIAL CONVENOR

The social convenor, together with the other executives, plans, organizes, promotes, and carries out social activities for the choir.

1. He originates ideas for activities.
2. He determines whether there is sufficient interest among the choir members to make an activity enjoyable for most of them.
3. He arranges for facilities, equipment, food, transportation, personnel, and anything else that may be required to promote good will and fellowship within the choir.

EDITOR OF THE CHOIR NEWSLETTER

1. The editor of the choir newsletter[5] arranges for the

[5]Some possible titles for the choir newsletter are *Choir Beat, Choir Notes, The Grapevine, News and Notes,* and *Notebook.*

gathering of material and for the paste-up and printing of a monthly choir newsletter, which should contain, at various times, some or all of the following:

A. Encouragement to faithfulness
B. Thanks for faithfulness
C. Directions from the conductor
D. Anecdotes and humorous stories
E. Articles on theory, articles on voice production, hymn stories, and so forth
F. Information about different choir members
G. Information about upcoming events for the choir

2. He distributes the newsletter monthly, at a regular choir rehearsal.

Parents' Guild

Members of the parents' guild assist the directors of the junior and younger choirs.

1. They discipline during rehearsals as necessary.
2. They assist with robing for performances.
3. They provide transportation on outings.
4. They promote and support the choir.
5. They assist with fund-raising activities, according to the custom of the local church.

Interpersonal Relationships in the Music Program

Senior minister and minister of music

The senior minister is the shepherd of the local church. Therefore, all persons and things in the church are under both his responsibility and his authority. He is the immediate supervisor of all other staff members, including the minister of music. The senior minister and the minister of music should hold a common philosophy of ministry, a common doctrinal standard, and a common philosophy concerning method of operation. The senior minister should have a clear understanding of the music program and of the goals and objectives of the minister of music. The minister of music is presumably more expert in the field of music than the senior minister is; so he functions as a resource person to the senior minister and, in point of fact, runs the music department of the church. The two men's responsibilities must not overlap in any area. They should publicly support one another for the good of the whole ministry. If there are differences of opinion, the two men should discuss them freely and candidly behind closed doors as responsible executives of the church of Jesus Christ. There must be complete freedom of communication between them. This is not duplicity or "politics" but simply courtesy and discretion. They should take every care to guard and support each other and the other staff members.

Minister of Music and Choir Directors

The minister of music is the choir directors' supervisor, trainer, resource person, and guide in the music ministry of the church. He should encourage, exhort where necessary, and disciple these people, who are under his direction and responsibility.

Minister of Music and Accompanists

The minister of music presumably is not an expert in all facets of musical expression, but as he is able, he should train, guide, and encourage the church accompanists. He should always be alert to their choices of music, styles and manners of dress, playing, and lives. He should exhort where necessary and lovingly lead them into a more mature level of performance skills and Christian living.

Minister of Music and Music Committee

The music committee is the administrative arm of the music department. Its functions are numerous and vital. The minister of music is the leading catalyst of the music committee and its main resource and help. Its members are his main assistants. They do much of the legwork required for a smoothly running program, and they assist him in making many of the executive decisions that are best done on a committee level. (For example, it would be good to have the music committee assist the minister of music in the decision to relieve an unsuitable director or accompanist of his duties. Such committee assistance relieves the possibility of ill will between the person removed and the minister of music, because the administration—not the minister of music—will have made the decision.)

Minister of music and platform committee

The minister of music should always inform the platform committee well in advance of any changes from the ordinary music in any of the church services. He then provides guidance about stage appearance, microphones required for soloists, and so forth.

Minister of music and worship committee

The minister of music serves as a resource person for the worship committee.

Minister of music and audiovisual committee

The minister of music serves as an advisor to the audiovisual committee in matters regarding the best adjustments and settings for the sound system in order to obtain the musical and acoustical effect that he thinks is best. The effect desired, and thus the adjustments and settings required, will vary from person to person and group to group, depending on the number of people involved, their projection, their vocal clarity, the building design, the system capabilities, and so forth.

Minster of music and Christian education committee

The minister of music may be asked to teach some or all of the music courses in the Christian education department, depending on his expertise and his available time. He may also serve as a resource person in the acquisition of musical materials, accompanists, or special music for the Christian education department.

Directors and accompanists

The director of any music group is totally responsible, under the minister of music or the music committee or both, for that particular group. He is the leader, and the instrumentalists are to follow his lead, or, more accurate musically, *accompany* his lead.

Music committee and all music personnel

The music committee is to make recommendations to the church board for all the leadership positions within the music department. This committee is the administrative arm of the music program, and its members must constantly evaluate the program and all its participants. As the administrative council, this committee is responsible for ensuring quality in all areas of the music program. Discipline, careful selection of soloists and other special music, and care of the ministry are part of its members' responsibility. Operating under the direction and guidance of the minister of music, this committee is responsible for the entire department and all that the department does.

4

Musical Groups in the Church

In this chapter, some general comments on purpose (or function), needs, and personnel will be followed by a considered look at each of the musical groups in a church individually. The chapter concludes with a brief overview of an extended executive group that includes some of the roles outlined in chapter two. (Such an executive group is appropriate in a large church, but it could conceivably be a part of a smaller church as well. In a smaller church, having an executive group can be a way of involving more people in positions of responsibility, or it can be a way of using fewer people by combining responsibilities.)

Purpose

The purpose of any musical group is multifaceted. The purpose of the group is not simply to perform music. In a Christian musical group, one purpose is the fulfillment of the obligations of service through offering worship, extending the Kingdom through evangelism, and building up the body of Christ through discipleship, or teaching. A second purpose of a musical group is the ministry of the participants to each other. Encouragement, comfort, exhortation, and fellowship become a very real benefit of meeting together to rehearse or perform. (A note of explanation is in order here. We do not practice and then worship, or practice and then serve. *All* that we do is ministry. The term *performance* is therefore used in this book to designate a public presentation as defined in *FUNK &*

WAGNALLS STANDARD COLLEGE DICTIONARY, New Updated Edition.) A third function of a musical group is socialization. Man is a social being, so he must socialize. Strength and meaning are found in group participation, and particularly by membership in something the individual considers significant. It should be remembered that these needs are met in the normal group settings, but that they are enhanced by other supportive endeavors like recreational activities, Bible study groups, associations built on interests or hobbies, and so on. All a person's needs are to be met in the body of Christ. Let us guard against spiritualizing musical groups to the neglect of the whole person.

Quality

Several factors determine both the quality and the usefulness of any group. There are the obvious factors like the average musical talent of the group, rehearsal time, and the like, but there are other factors that are equally as important. As already mentioned, the strength that comes from fellowship and simply getting to know each other well is a contributing force in determining the value of the group's service. Moreover, it should be noted that the group will not rise above the level of several other determining factors, which are listed below:

1. The competence of the director
2. The talent, dedication, efficiency, and faithfulness of the individual members
3. The challenge presented to the group members:
   A. Are they *expected* to improve?
   B. Does the music stretch their abilities?
   C. Are their sights constantly directed to the mature Christian life?
   D. Does a large percentage of the group accept personal responsibility for the group? A director or leader can only move with persons who are willing to move. If the leader spends all his time trying to motivate the masses, very little may be accomplished. Not everyone will

move; not everyone will rise to a challenge. Surely there must be an honest attempt to motivate the masses to become movers, but the bulk of any leader's energy should be directed at guiding and encouraging those who are on the march for God and His music. Those who are self-motivated are those who will respond easiest to the leader. It is therefore wise to use those who are motivated to motivate the others. Every individual is important and will benefit from guidance and concern.

Personnel

Two concluding points must be added to these general comments; one concerns auditions for membership, the other concerns discipline.

Auditions for membership

First, who should get into the various musical groups of the church? There are the obvious factors such as musical ability, general mental and physical health, and Christian commitment; and beyond those factors the decisions will vary from church to church, depending on each church's philosophy and aims for its group. The question of auditions is often a thorn to members and directors alike; it need not be. A simple audition (which is sometimes less threatening if it is called a "visit," a "chat," a "discussion," a "little sing," or something similar) can accomplish many things for the director and can have benefits for the member as well. The director can learn the person's general musical ability and his willingness to be faithful; and if a longer and more in-depth audition is held, the director can learn much more.

For a "first ever" series of auditions for a senior choir, the director should consider the following instructions as an example:

1. The director should have the person sing the melody of a very familiar hymn while the director accompanies him simply on the piano.

2. The director should have the person sing the part he usually sings (sopranos sing the alto part) while the director accompanies him.

Those two items are all that are generally necessary. They are enough to determine if the person can sing at all, and if he can read at all.

If, however, the person is not nervous and seems relaxed enough to be more thoroughly examined; or if the director is looking for soloists, members for a special group, or so forth and suspects that this person has the capacity to fulfill the role; or if the person fails to complete steps one and two satisfactorily, the director may wish to add the following steps:

3. The director should have the person auditioning run through some standard vocal exercises to determine range, control, pitch, and texture of the voice. Five-note ascending and descending scales on a simple *ah* vowel work nicely.
4. The director should sing a part while the person auditioning sings the melody and vice versa. This exercise will assist the director in determining the person's ability to hold his own in a small group. Also, it is likely that one who does well on this exercise will be able to keep from wavering if someone beside him sings off-key occasionally. The person who does well here is the kind of person to put behind or beside a "follower" or a weaker singer.
5. The director should have a person read through a moderately difficult anthem to determine his sight-reading skill.

The director should remember to use only the first two steps unless conditions indicate otherwise. Many of the group members have never had to undergo an audition and will be extremely nervous. No one must feel that he would rather quit than be auditioned, but everyone should participate in it. (Note: Some directors use an audition only when a problem person needs to be dismissed. Auditioning everyone, say once a year or when he joins, will first of all prevent such a person from getting into the group to start with. Second, if everyone is or has been auditioned, the problem person will not feel picked on.)

Once the director has determined each person's level of competence as accurately as he can, he should record it in that person's personal file. This file should include the person's name, address, home and work telephone numbers, voice part, range, classification (coloratura, lyric, dramatic, mezzo, and so forth), and comments on attitudes and other musical skills (instruments played, performance history, and so forth). This file is not the one the secretary-treasurer uses for recording attendance; rather, it is to be kept confidential by the director and the minister of music.

The benefits that the director and the total program can gain from auditions are obvious. The director can now accurately arrange his seating plan, make recommendations to the music committee regarding soloists and people to try in small groups, and so on. How, though, will auditions benefit the poor "victim"?

1. The person auditioning will, for at least once in his life, have sung alone, in spite of his apprehensions
2. He can now be placed in a seating arrangement that will be most beneficial to himself and to the group.
3. He may have felt capable of singing in a small group or as a soloist but had been too shy to ask and had not yet been discovered by the director or by the music committee.
4. The person may not have felt capable of having such a solo or group ministry but may indeed have the ability and can now be led into a new and exciting phase in the development of his personal ministry.
5. The person may be incapable of public group singing and will be saved needless embarrassment by being told so immediately, not after some weeks or indeed years of unknowingly being a disturbance or an object of pity. A word of caution here: The director should not suggest by name another ministry that he thinks an unsuccessful applicant might try. By making a specific suggestion, the director

may just be creating a problem for both the unsuccessful applicant and the leader of the other program, should it happen that the unsuccessful applicant cannot fit into that program either. The choir director should suggest that the unsuccessful applicant try another field of service, but he should not name anything specifically. If, however, the director feels that the person could function well in a specific area, he should tell the leader of that area and let him approach the person himself if he wishes to pursue it.

One final suggestion regarding auditions: Children are best tested when two or three of them can sing together. The audition is less threatening that way.

Discipline

The second item dealing with personnel is the matter of discipline. Each age group has its unique problems, and many of them are dealt with expertly in books like Ruth Krehbiel Jacobs' *The Children's Choir* (Philadelphia: Fortress, 1958). Here we shall consider only the ground rules for maintaining discipline in any group, though each group will have unique goals, members, and problems for which these ground rules may be modified.

1. Maintaining discipline is easier than enforcing it.
2. A unified group desire to cooperate in reaching a specific goal is invaluable.
3. The leader should hold the group's attention and keep everyone busy. He should avoid working with one section for longer than a couple of minutes, if that is at all possible.
4. He should make the entire experience enjoyable. If he enjoys the work and the people, his good attitude will do much to promote the group's enjoyment as well.
5. His positive attitude should be reflected in his comments about life, his relationship to God, and the ministry he has, as well as in the particular piece of music being worked on.
6. He should build up and encourage individuals by name.

7. He should respect the individuals in his group.
8. He should be vitally involved and enthusiastic about working on the music with the group.
9. From this base, he should encourage in the group an attitude of wanting to learn and develop.
10. Once an attitude of wanting to learn and develop is begun, he can challenge the people in the group to do their best.
11. He should know what he wants in sound, attitude, and behavior; *tell* the group exactly what he expects; then demand it.
12. He should pray much for and with the group and the individuals in it, expressing his dependence on Christ.

Basic Musical Groups in a Graded Choir Program

And now just a few brief comments on each of the regular groups that form the core of any church music program.

Senior choir

The most important group in local church music is the senior choir. This group has many important functions, but people often overlook or ignore the fact that the senior choir is the visible sign of life in any music program. The lack of a senior choir is perhaps the most noticed event that can occur in a service, outside of the pastor's not showing up. Every local church that hosts a public worship service is expected to have one. Again the question of validity arises: Is it valid to organize a senior choir just because one is expected? The answer can only be no, if it is assumed that *expected* means expected by other people. If, however, expected means expected by the church itself—that is, those who wish to be participants in a senior choir as an avenue of service—the answer must be yes. The senior choir, if it is the only regularly functioning group in the church, may be made up of persons from high school age and up. If, however, a good youth choir program is in operation, the senior choir should be limited to persons of college age and older.

The senior choir's main function is to lead in worship, and the members of the choir will perform this function most effectively if they themselves are worshiping. Through the presentation of their anthems, a call to worship, and a prayer response, they speak to the congregation for God and respond to God for the congregation. Their repertoire should be varied and within their ability to perform well. It really is better for them to do three-part, two-part, or unison music well than for them to do a sloppy job of a four-, six-, or eight-part anthem. Simplicity is not a trend of the day, whereas the showy or extravagant is. Let us do the most we can in the best and most appropriate way possible and with the greatest degree of competence possible—because the God whom we say that we honor and serve deserves nothing less.

Much effort has been expended in this book to point everyone to the goal of a biblical unity of purpose and philosophy. Much energy is expended in practice sessions aimed at achieving a unified sound. The one obvious area of consideration that remains is the presentation of a uniform appearance. The question of choir gowns, seating arrangements based on height, music folders versus individual pieces of music, lighting, positioning, and so on are all aspects of a consideration of visibility. We shall now consider each of those areas briefly, underlining their importance to a public ministry.

Gowns. Should the members of the senior choir wear choir gowns or not? And if gowns should be worn, what kind of gown is best?

I favor the use of gowns for the senior choir and for any other choir for these reasons, among others that may be named:

1. Gowns add dignity.
2. They add uniformity.
3. They assure equality of appearance, despite real inequalities in economic status and attire, thus limiting the fashion-show syndrome.

4. They provide a cover-up in the event of minor mishaps on the way to church (picking up a child who has muddy feet, for instance).

Some cautions are in order here:

1. Gowns should be made of a fairly lightweight material that breathes well, yet not a material so light as to lose its shape.
2. The style and color should not only blend with the other colors in the building but also fit the character of the church. Flamboyant metallic robes do not suit an ultraconservative congregation.
3. There should be a budget entry for dry cleaning once a year, and more often if necessary.

Seating. Aesthetically pleasing seating arrangements are also important; yet I said earlier that a strong singer should be seated behind or beside a weak singer. Both factors must be considered, the latter getting priority.

As a general rule, the strongest voices should be at the back of the group, the soft, pleasant voices should be at the front, and the rest should be in between. Thus the strong, sure singers can "sing through" the others, assisting them in carrying the part; the singers in front, the ones with soft, pleasant voices, will be the ones most likely to be picked up by a poorly placed or poor quality microphone; and the singers who remain need not take offense that they are not in a favored position; rather, they should have the confidence that comes by osmosis from the singers surrounding them. After the choir members have been arranged by voice, they can be arranged according to height in their sections.

A seating plan similar to that in the following illustration is often useful in church choirs in which the ladies outnumber the men, causing a sound imbalance if the men are in the traditional positions behind the ladies' sections.

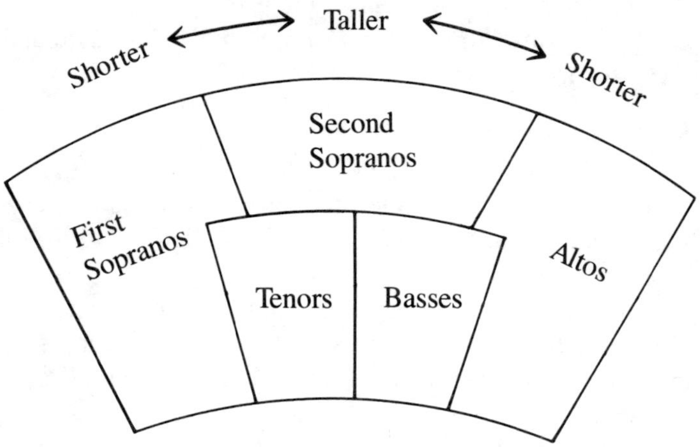

For a larger group of better singers, this more traditional arrangement may be preferred:

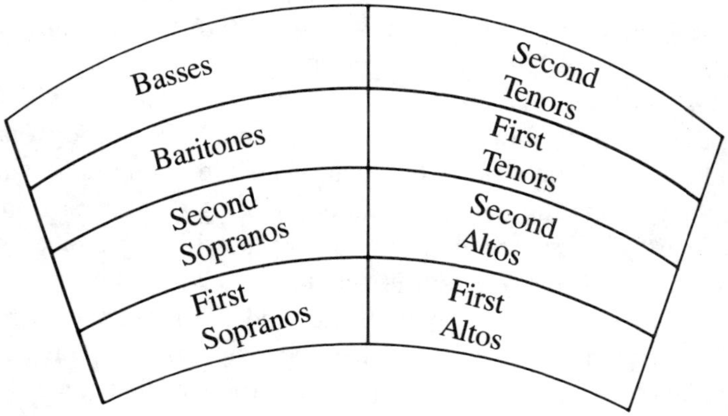

Folders. Another matter of appearance that is often debated is that of folders versus simple (and possibly ragged), individual pieces of music. I suggest the use of folders, for these reasons:

1. The obvious virtue of uniformity of appearance, not

within the group, of course, but from week to week
2. The steadying value of a hard cover rather than a single sheet of paper
3. A means for screening the members' orders of service, notes of instructions, and so forth from the rest of the congregation
4. The saving of the music from excess wear and tear (and bending, folding, spindling, or mutilation)

Lighting. The use of lighting effects, staging, and such things is now in vogue. I am in favor of using any honorable means of enhancing the message and encouraging a positive reception of it. If, however, the use of these extras takes away from a concentration on the message and leaves only a circus-like thrill in its place, the bounds of appropriateness have been overstepped. This problem need not occur, however, if there is a judicial exercise of common sense and a taste for simplicity. The extras must add to the message of the music, not displace it.

Placement. Placement of the choir is a constant question when new buildings are being planned. Cathedral style has a divided choir in the chancel, where the conductor directs from a place out of public view via a mirror. Other building styles place the choir in a loft at the rear of the sanctuary. Still others place the choir at the front and center of the sanctuary; in this arrangement, the conductor stands with his back to the congregation. Although some people object to the "public display" of this latter position, it is probably the best. In this placement, the vocal sound is directed out toward the other members of the congregation, who are the main recipients of the message. Any other positioning mentioned will necessitate their receiving reflected sound only.

YOUTH CHOIR

Two trends in youth choirs are common today, and each trend is all too often exclusive. Either young people prepare and perform a musical or a concert-tour program, or they serve regularly in the local church, usually in the evening service. Most senior choirs prepare both a cantata of sorts for Christmas, Easter, or Thanksgiving and their regular anthems, but youth choirs often seem to miss out on the enriching experience of doing both. If one must choose, though, the regular, faithful ministry to the choir's own local church is much to be preferred. In that ministry, the individuals learn the value and importance of steady, dependable participation in their program; they get a steady, concentrated diet of the Word from one pastor's teaching; and they have an opportunity to be a constant encouragement and challenge to the other members of their own congregation.

Characteristics of youth. Youth must press. They must have things to achieve, expectations to meet. Such activity is part of the experience of maturing. Youth will strive for mastery if properly motivated to do so, but they will rebel at any feeling of being controlled against their will. The line between proper motivation and too much control is fine, and it is obscured by youth's diverse reactions. Adolescents twelve to fourteen, for example, are extremely vulnerable. The physical changes they are undergoing produce a lack of coordination, voice change, self-consciousness, and a general lack of energy. To understand those characteristics and operate within them is fully half the battle when dealing with youth of this age. Bell choirs and instruments with controlled pitch are good to use at this age. Although boys and bells may not always mix, boys and pianos, organs, drums, marimbas, xylophones, and the like often mix with astonishingly good results.

High schoolers, by contrast, thrive on the discipline of regular responsibilities. They should not just practice; they need to perform. (Please note: The director should be courteous and post a performance schedule six months in advance if he can.) The director should remember that youth need variety in all that they do. For a youth choir to sing one song a month, with weekly rehearsals, is just plain bad news for the longevity of the program. Moreover, because of their growing independence it is wise for the director not to sing along with a youth choir (not that directors *should* sing with any choir, but it is tempting to do so with youth or children). He should also avoid the temptation to try to get as big a sound out of a youth choir as he could out of an adult choir. The youth simply do not have the capacity, and forcing the sound from them could be hazardous to their health.

Three other points:

1. The director should watch carefully the content and style of the music. Chapter five, "Determining Appropriateness," has more to say on this point.
2. He should avoid insipid group names like "The Gospel Melodaires" or "The I'm Bound for Glory Singers." Concentrated effort should be put into finding a group name only if there is a good reason for the group's not being known as "the youth choir from Grace Church," for example. A name like that seems to indicate quite well who the group is, what it does, and where it is from—what more could another name do?
3. He should teach attitudes and techniques of worship, discipleship, and evangelism. He should promote and reward disciplined lives and superior effort. He should encourage excellence, and if he has any discipline problems, he should deal with them individually and privately. Youth are easily wounded in front of their peers, and a director can totally lose young people's support if he should so destroy their self-esteem.

Here are some further items of importance regarding intermediates and seniors: Intermediates are in a time of physical change, emotional change, personality change, attitudinal change, and ability change. The watchword is *caution*. At this time of life, a total adult behavior pattern is being molded. Note: It is not just "happening." It is being molded. A very significant part of this molding is done in the area of music. At this time of life, training and work are most important; but those things are least desirable as far as the intermediates are concerned. For them, the thing of the moment is everything; and if something takes work and patience, they say "Forget it."

It is imperative that intermediates be told about and understand the changes that are taking place, and they must also be told about and understand that the changes happen to all of them, boys and girls. At this time of life, the entire voice box and supporting muscles change. These new developments must be understood and cared for. The new muscle forms are naturally weaker than those the person is accustomed to using and can be permanently damaged extremely easily.

The voice change is most noticeable in boys, because of the range variations, but girls undergo a lesser range alteration plus a maturing of the voice. Both boys' voices and girls' voices become huskier and not so pure and sweet. The male range narrows drastically from an average range of fifteen notes down to a possible five or six notes. Music to be used for this age group must be rewritten, and the boys and girls must be cautioned not to sing loudly, not to sing beyond a comfortable range, and not to yell during this time of voice change.

Intermediates despise hypocrisy and sham. Their director, therefore, must be sincere in his concern for them and for their musical futures. This is the most critical period, for now the chance is greatest that a person will become nonmusical if his abilities are not nurtured.

The interest in recorded music reaches its peak during these years. At this time, the intermediate's ability to hear and understand very complicated rhythms, pitch variations, and color changes increases. But it is also at this time that he is least likely to be able to reproduce what he can hear and understand. Therefore, he turns to recorded music as an outlet for what he is frustrated about not being able to do.

During adolescence, the whole person is changing. The adolescent's body is haywire, and so is the adolescent's attitude and performance. The frustration of self-consciousness about things he does not understand and things he cannot do demands extra sensitivity on the part of the director. Adolescents are changing from children into adults, and they must not be treated like children.

Again, the watchword is *caution*.

Emphasize participation more than performance. As has already been stated, the intermediate can now hear almost any complicated music pattern and will quickly learn to imitate it as soon as his abilities to perform catch up to his ability to hear. When those two abilities mesh, the music student now has full *potential*. He cannot do it yet, but the potential is there. Range is one example. Every singer has a potential range, when he reaches vocal maturity, far greater than is generally accepted. Because of the lack of understanding on the part of choir directors and voice teachers, this potential is almost never realized. There are two opposite and equally harmful practices in existence today: one is pushing the young voice as high and as low as possible, and as fast as possible; the other is taking the path of least resistance and making no effort at all to expand the ranges. Young adult sopranos who sing G above high C—or even higher—and down to the contralto G need not be a rarity. Contraltos with a free, usable high C, tenors with a low A flat and a high D flat, baritones with an F to B flat range, and basses who can sing a low B flat and a tenor G could all be relatively frequent among well-trained amateurs as well as among professionals.

Much of the damage in range is done in the years between fourteen and eighteen, when attitudes and physical, mental, and emotional habits are so firmly ingrained that their later adjustment becomes difficult if not impossible. Let us examine the following chart of ranges for high school students:

	High School	Tessitura (More Usable Range)
Soprano	B-B (2 oct.)	F-D (¾ oct.)
Alto	A-E (1½ oct.)	C-A (¾ oct.)
Tenor	C-E (1⅓ oct.)	E-C (¾ oct.)
Baritone	A-D (1⅓ oct.)	C-A (¾ oct.)
Bass	E-C (1⅔ oct.)	A-G (⅞ oct.)

These ranges are idealistic but possible; if they were pared by about a quarter to a third, they would be more of a reflection of the average. Too many people, when their voice has changed, develop a psychological reaction I call "I can't hit it-itis." If the top of the range, which is the most easily lost, is worked and retained, the lower registers will develop. Use of the high voice should be constantly encouraged, but the voice should go only as high as is comfortable. The voice should *never* be strained.

All too often persons who can harmonize or read music are made to sing bass or alto when they should sing tenor or soprano. Very often those people, had they been encouraged to use their natural ranges, could now be singing much higher and possibly much lower. Forcing a voice into a mold limits it on both ends.

Because this period is one of extremely sharp senses and abilities, it is an excellent time for original composition or arranging. Such work should be encouraged, even if the results do not seem good. Even professionals pump out hundreds of so-so pieces for every hit. Neither a voice nor a writer should ever be confined, squeezed, forced or driven, though guidance and help are valuable.

Small groups for intermediate singers should not be mixed, simply because of the voice variations. Trios, quartets, sextets, and so forth can be organized at this time, but they should be kept all male or all female. Real encouragement and enjoyment can come from these groups, especially for girls. Boys some-

[1]From Madeline Ingram and William C. Rice, *Vocal Technique for Children and Youth* (Nashville: Abingdon, 1962).

times function better in a chorus. It is interesting that boys from grades four through eight or nine will work well together, but a girls' group should not span more than two or three years. Parts become an increasingly simple thing for intermediates and should be introduced, but attention should be paid to who sings what.

Some students may not have had any prior training and will say that they cannot sing. It is interesting to note that the only person who cannot sing is the true monotone—that is, someone who sings one note all the time. Anyone who can vary the pitch of his voice can be trained to sing. Someone who cannot carry a pitch can be taught—with love and patience—if the teacher has the ability and time to teach him.

There is often a marked change between grade eight students and grade nine students. The grade nine students are more developed, more capable, and more mature and interested—sometimes amazingly more so.

Breathing, relaxation, head tone, pitch, phrasing, diction, articulation, and support are all things that intermediates have the ability to learn and do at this time. Future choirs, and the students who are now intermediates, will benefit from what they are now taught. It should also be noted that many public schools have excellent music programs in both instrumental and choral music. This benefit should be capitalized on and the people trained in public schools should be used as a base for church work.

Mixed groups should be introduced at the high school level.

Music and performance for intermediates and seniors. Some points about music and performance for intermediates and seniors follow.

Good music is not always difficult and difficult music is not always good. So what makes good music? First, all music is not good for all groups—the music must fit the group. Then consider:

1. Are the words biblically sound?
2. Does the tune fit the words?

3. Is the piece well written musically?
4. Is the piece interesting musically?
5. What atmosphere does the piece create?

Light, meaningless texts should be avoided, unless they are for a specific purpose. People at this age can assimilate and appreciate the finest lyrics.

Old favorites are good to use, contrary to what is commonly held. Contemporary songs are also excellent, if they meet the above criteria. A song that asks a question but provides no answer only confuses. Do not use it.

The desire to involve as many people as possible is greatly aided by the number of people who, by this time, could be becoming very proficient on instruments. Many schools have quite good instruction in recorder, for example, which is a very good instrument for obligato or doubled accompaniment. If piano students are available they should be used. The same holds true for people who are learning any instrument—they should be used.

An excellent opportunity for performance practice is in the younger departments of the Sunday school. Talk about an eager audience! The youth will gain experience and recognition, and they will benefit the Sunday school as well.

The music chosen must encourage the intermediates to sing and participate when they are at the stage of life when involvement is not popular. As much as is possible, the youth groups must be used in regular services, not just at Easter and Christmas. The intermediate age is the age when churches have dropouts. Regular participation in a quality music program will help keep youth coming to church. Interesting, quality music should be chosen.

Teaching plan. A youth choir director should decide what he would like to teach and how he intends to teach it. First and foremost, he should teach by example. If he wants his students to be active, dedicated Christian musicians—he should be one himself.

He should teach basic music; that is, he should teach what

pitch is, what 𝄐 and ♪ mean, what the difference between 𝄻 and 𝄼 is, and what <, dim., rit., ♯, DS., Dal Capo, and so forth mean so that his people know what they are doing. He should not attempt to cover everything at once; he should cover things a little at a time as they come up, putting particular emphasis on basic terms and signs. He should establish a plan of what he wishes to cover in a year and follow it.

He should also teach stewardship of God's possessions. If a person belongs to God, then that person is God's possession. One's talent is to be developed and used for God's glory. It is an obligation, not an option. God expects one's best.

As much as the director is able, he should teach proper vocal technique.

He should also teach stage manner—how to relax in front of an audience—because this is the age when people should be taught to sing solos and participate in small groups.

Finally, he should teach his students to pray for each other, for the group, and for their director.

Suggestions for the director. Here are some general suggestions that may prove helpful to the director:

1. If a singer is uncertain:
   A. Is he really listening to what he hears?
   B. Is he really trying? Is he really doing his best?
   C. Is he thinking, or is he "just singing"?
   D. He should be surrounded—especially from behind—with stronger singers who sing the same part.
2. Intermediates and seniors respond to suggestions better than they respond to orders.
3. The director should make positive statements about a better way to do something rather than give out negative criticism.
4. Knowledge of individual people is invaluable.
5. The director should not be sarcastic in discipline; he should be fair and treat everyone equally in the matter of discipline.

6. The director should encourage the members of his group to place Christ first in their lives and thus get more meaning from what they sing.
7. The director should choose anthems and hymns that are colorful, emotional, idealistic, and have missionary and personal application. The music chosen should show the power and majesty of God.
8. The director should be able and willing to counsel the members of his group about their physical changes and needs, their emotional adjustments, and their relationship to Jesus Christ.
9. The director should make practices varied and never too long. People in a tired choir will not perform well, and their parents may get upset as well.

The director. A man is the best choice for a director in this age group, though a talented woman is preferable to a mediocre man. The director should be someone who is at ease, accurate in rhythm and pitch, and able to vary the music selected. He should be a good leader, a punctual person, and so on, as discussed in chapter two, "Qualifications of Personnel in the Music Program."

Following is a list of things the director should be prepared to do:

1. He is responsible for music distribution, if necessary.
2. He must announce songs distinctly.
3. He should begin each rehearsal with a familiar song.
4. He should coordinate music with the theme of the day of performance, if there is one.
5. He will assure, well in advance, that the pianist knows the songs chosen.
6. He may make arrangements for special music.
7. He should teach new songs.
8. He should plan variety in the music program. A musical rut is just a grave with the ends knocked out.
9. He must notify a substitute in the event of his absence.
10. When he conducts, he should interpret the music so that it lives, both for the group and for the audience.

JUNIOR CHOIR

The next regular choir to be considered is the junior choir: grades four through six. The Chorister's Guild (P. O. Box 38188, Dallas, Texas 75238) has top quality information on this age group, and on younger children and those a little older as well. The emphasis, material for teaching, music, and promotional ideas of the Chorister's Guild are excellent.

Characteristics of juniors. Children in this age bracket are impressionable hero worshipers and boisterous "big kids" at school. They are beginning to be quite taken by members of the opposite sex, and they generally have a very severe case of the "normals." They can learn anything but will need help in finding their voice. Their upper range is still their natural voice, but the boys may want to sing like dad, not like mom. Their upper range can be expanded, and for most of them it will settle at about an octave and a half. Volume should not be forced—the juniors' muscles are incapable of forced volume over extended periods without damage. The temptation to try to make a children's choir sound like an adult choir must be avoided.

Great things should be expected from juniors. They should be challenged to do well, but they should not be forced to do things they are not physically able to do. The director must be careful not to treat them "like the little kids"; such treatment is definitely not appreciated. They are capable of much; as a result, much should be expected of them and they should be told that much is expected of them. The director should be explicit in all his instructions to them—he should not expect them to do what they have not been told how to do. This group is at the peak of childhood; and if a younger group cannot be formed to feed this one, juniors are the ones to begin musical training with.

Teaching plan. Basic theory should be taught during rehearsals as opportunities arise: it should not be taught as a textbook topic. However, the director should try to establish a plan of material to cover each year in order to ensure uniformity throughout the program. The group should progress from unison singing to rounds, then to two-part harmony, and maybe even to three-part harmony. Once the songs are mastered, they should be used. Regular, worthwhile performances are imperative both for the ministry they can provide and for the singers' own satisfaction and development. As the juniors learn more songs, they should be taught good posture and diction by the director's constant example and by his words. Tone production, phrasing, pitch, and so forth should all be communicated the same way: the director should be both a teacher and a working model of what his students are to be. The importance of the Christian life, the importance of ministry through music, and the importance of the meanings of the texts all become real when demonstrated continuously in the director's genuine Christian life and explained occasionally by him. He should always remember that juniors want genuineness.

It always strengthens each group if activities between groups are coordinated. If this choir can grow out of the Christian education department through either the Sunday school or a club, both the choir and the group it came from will be bolstered. Care should be exercised to ensure that there is *only* cooperation—the groups must be free from conflicts of interest and conflicts in scheduling, not only for practices but for performances, social outings, and the like as well.

Music. One point about the texts of the music for junior choir must be made. Children of this age group, like those younger, are not yet future conscious. Songs emphasizing God's present grace will be much more meaningful than those of eternal reward. And a final point about accompaniment. Often the juniors are learning instruments and can supply much of the accompaniment themselves. They are also at the age at which they are beginning to listen to music on the radio and elsewhere and are able to handle more complex rhythms; so such rhythms need not be avoided, as they must with primary choirs.

A final note. If the director is interested in the members of his junior choir as people, they will gain an interest in the music. If the director wins the right to be heard, his choir members will listen. If he demand their interest and their attention without deserving either, his choir members will (quite impolitely) ignore him.

Specialty Musical Groups in a Graded Choir Program

Specialty choirs are those that not every church can muster; they are the spice in the program. Included in this list are the next younger children's group, the primary choir (children in grades one to three), and a preschool choir (the four- and five-year-olds who love to sing and play). A more advanced group than the senior choir represents the other end of the scale. This group is sometimes referred to as the chancel choir. In between would be the men's and ladies' choruses, Sunday school class choirs, youth club choirs, senior citizens' choirs, and any other of the more or less regularly functioning ensembles of the church. Any groups that do not function regularly would also come under this heading. Groups like a choir made up of several families for a series of meetings on family living could be useful and a further emphasis—usually—of the theme of the meetings.

The possibilities for occasional specialty groups are almost endless. A group of teachers could sing at the next Christian education conference. The men who lead the boys' club could form a male chorus once in a while. There need not be a "deep spiritual" use for the choir: it may exist merely to perform a fun song, or it may be used to teach. Music, like everything else in the Christian life, must be honoring to the character of God and must speak to the whole man, not just his Sunday-morning side.

A few suggestions regarding some of these specialty groups are appropriate here. More is said about the primary choir than about other specialty choirs because the primary choir usually has a greater similarity to a regular choir than do the other specialty choirs named.

PRIMARY CHOIR

Characteristics of primary children. Primary children are the show-offs of the human race. They are very sensitive to disapproval and respond well to praise. Because of their need to be recognized, they develop vivid imaginations and tend to dramatize everything. Primary years are a time of development and fast learning; thus these years present a tremendous opportunity for primary children to learn good music. Children of this age enjoy life and can enjoy learning music.

Although their voice ranges vary greatly, primary children generally can go from about C to F. Primaries can sing almost anything, but the most usable range is from three notes above the bottom to three notes below the top (E to D). Their voices should not be strained on either end: a strain either way will cause equal harm. Primaries are not capable of marked dynamic changes, so they should not even be attempted. These children have the ability to sing, but they probably lack the knowledge, which the director can supply.

Music. The songs chosen should be simple songs of only one verse. They must have a clear meaning that the children can understand.

Primary children are extremely active. This energy should be employed by the use of music involving action and motion. Such music will use up some of the children's energy and help teach them rhythmic expression.

It is good to teach primaries some hymns. *Care* is the byword when choosing hymns: make sure that the hymn fits the need. Some good examples are:

1. "Thy Word Is like a Garden, Lord"
2. "Fairest Lord Jesus"
3. "Savior, like a Shepherd Lead Us"
4. "Stand up for Jesus"
5. "I'm a Child of the King"
6. "Joyful, Joyful, We Adore Thee"

Two bad examples are "Rock of Ages" and "O Sacred

Head, Now Wounded.'' Phrases such as ''Here I raise mine Ebeneezer'' just will not do. They are beyond the child's comprehension.

The music progressions must be simple. Small jumps are preferable to close steps because they are easier to hear. Young children cannot always distinguish between small pitch differences.

Make sure that the words and music say the same thing. These questions should be asked when pieces are being selected:

1. Is the subject matter of value and interest to the children?
2. Is the rhythm strong and vital? Children are not accurate time keepers, so the stronger the beat the better.
3. Is the song the kind that the children will want to sing after they have learned it and are on their own?
4. Is the music good music? It is important to remember that the children's musical tastes are being built.

Performances. Primary children should be used at regular services, be they Sunday school, junior church, or worship services, not just at Christmas and Easter services. Primaries should be used as a group (department) or in small groups to encourage them and expose them to performance.

Teaching plan. Fun songs and action songs should be used. Enjoyment in music at each practice should be a goal.

Music can be used as a teaching tool to:

1. Emphasize a point in a lesson
2. Prepare for worship
3. Assist in the act of worship
4. Quiet and unite the children (that is, if the primaries are ''all over the place'' both physically and in their attention, it is a good time for them to sing; their attention will be regained and they will be united)

Visual aids should be used to teach a song. Bulletin boards, blackboards, overhead projectors, and so forth are all great.

(For example, a garden scene can be shown for "Thy Word Is like a Garden, Lord"; a flock of sheep with a good shepherd can be shown for "Savior, like a Shepherd Lead Us"; and the children can march to "Stand up for Jesus.")

The words and music should always be taught together. They are a song, not words and music.

Generally, teaching should be by rote (imitation) rather than by note, but music should always be used. Children do not learn to read without words, nor should they learn to sing without music.

Children should not be taught by the accompaniment. They should be taught by singing; then the piano can be added quietly.

Participation should be emphasized more than performance.

The equipment used must be of top quality. Pianos and other instruments must be in tune and in repair. Children cannot learn accurate music from poor equipment.

Children will imitate the director's posture, breathing, enunciation, and song interpretation. He does not need to mention those matters unless warranted. Because the children will naturally mimic him, he should look sharp! Some good periodicals include:

1. *Music Makers*
2. *The Church Musician*
3. *The Music Leader* (all three of which are available from the Sunday School Board of the Southern Baptist Convention, 127 Ninth Avenue North, Nashville, Tenn. 37234) and the Chorister's Guild *Letters* (available from the Chorister's Guild, P.O. Box 38188, Dallas, Tex. 75238).

The children should be allowed to lead on occasion, if they are capable. Motion and action should be used whenever possible. Rhythm should be steady. The director should enunciate clearly. Children's songs should never drag. The piano should be kept soft and simple, with the melody prominent. The children should be taught to pray for each other and for their director. Their attention span is very short; so style and songs should be changed often. In order to make an impression, it is necessary to repeat, repeat, repeat.

The director should not always sing along with the children. Letting them carry the singing by themselves gives the director a chance to listen and gives the children a chance to be independent.

All the children should be encouraged to take part, no matter how "out of tune" some of them may be—they *can* learn to sing.

Ensembles

Ensembles of various natures are a part of almost every church music program. Often a small church has one or more ensembles but no choir, simply because of the lack of a sufficient number of musical people to form a choir. Ensembles often require more faithfulness, diligence, and time than a larger group, and as a result they may prove to be of more value to the participants. These groups may be formally or informally begun, but they are made up of regular participants, though many individuals may be involved in several such groups.

Duets, trios, quartets, youth ensembles, and the like form the core of the special music of the church, along with the soloists used. Their ministry is significant, and it is often seen as a personal ministry rather than as a group ministry. These groups can provide much in the way of variety in sound, style, texture, and emphasis. The guidelines that regulate all the other music in the church should be kept in mind when guidelines are set for ensembles. These smaller groups function more or less independently, but they are still subject to the church's philosophy of ministry and to the direction of the minister of music and the music committee.

A further word of advice regarding ensemble music: Most untrained voices have a break, a note or two that are difficult to sing and at which the placement of the sound in the throat shifts. These breaks, of course, are undesirable, but they must be recognized and dealt with. Any arrangements for soloists or small groups should take the singers' breaks into consideration and try to avoid the problem notes in each person's part. Alterations that will degrade the music should not be made, and maintaining a flow is desirable in any piece of music. One word of caution: Any mention of a break to a singer will make him aware of it and usually cause it to be more pronounced; therefore, it is wise to work at alleviating the break without drawing attention to it.

Chancel choir

The chancel choir (or any other designation a church may use) is a group of the most expert singers of the church. Members of this choir are chosen for their voice quality, sight-reading skills, varied musical interests, and solid Christian commitment. They usually perform the more difficult works, which come from a variety of periods and are beyond the interests and skills of the senior choir. From motets to modern, they do it all, and they do it all well. Chancel choirs are seldom larger than twenty to twenty-four members. They can serve in concert ministries as well as in regular church services. Any broadcasting or recording ministries are likely to center on a church's chancel choir.

Choruses

Men's and ladies' choruses can have very effective ministries. Participants in such a chorus have much in common and find membership in the chorus to be a fulfilling and rewarding part of their lives—it often meets needs that would otherwise go unmet. Music is readily available for both men's and ladies' choruses: ladies' music is usually three-part and men's four-part. In addition to benefiting the participants, these choruses can have specialized areas of outreach. Christian businessmen's clubs and Christian women's clubs are always in need of good music that fits into their programs, and choruses are a natural choice for such ministries. Prison ministries, boys' or girls' clubs, service clubs, tours, festivals, and so on are all open to ministries from men's and ladies' choruses.

CLUB AND CLASS CHOIRS

Youth club and Sunday school class choirs are limited to members of those organizations. The same care should be taken with these groups as with the age-level choirs already mentioned. Club and class choirs often serve their members in a different way from the way a regular choir serves its members. Often these smaller group choirs offer enrichment to their members who otherwise might not be involved in music. The small choirs can promote an interest in music and can serve as media of service and expression perhaps not used before.

Practices will likely be during the regular group activities and thus will be limited in time and scope. They must be well planned, and they should be times for teaching both music and the Christian life. New hymns, part-singing if the group is ready, and proper attitudes toward worship and music should be taught. Bad music, like bad attitudes, will yield a tolerance for more of the same. Good music, like good attitudes, will open the door for more of the good.

Club and class choirs are good places to use stories about hymn origins, hymn authors and composers, and so forth from books like Clint Bonner's *A Hymn Is Born* (Nashville: Broadman, 1959). Hymns and anthems usually have the better teaching texts; so avoid choruses which are frivolous or in error. The singing of good hymns and anthems also provides opportunities for going over relevant biblical texts and presenting the Lord's claims on our lives. However, fun and action songs should be used as well.

Any other special group may be formed if there are enough participants. There is no need to worry about finding a place for such a group to sing in, for the places always outnumber the groups. One bit of advice on senior citizens' choirs: The music should be transposed down a minor third or so, depending on the group. The members will find it easier to sing, and others will find it more pleasing to listen to. Choirs from the men's fellowship, women's missions organization, Christian education workers, and homebuilders' club are all possibilities. The extent of participation is limited only by the number of people available, the amount of work put into the project, and the availability of a qualified director.

INSTRUMENTS

The growing use of instrumentalists in the church is opening up all sorts of exciting prospects. Children who have learned to play instruments at school deserve an outlet at church to use their abilities for God's glory among His gathered people. Many older people have participated in town or military bands and would love to perform again. The opportunities for using instrumentalists are as open-ended as those for vocalists, with the limitation that there are not as many instrumentalists.

The use of instruments in the church has a history that runs from the time of ancient Israel to the present. Individuals or a group of instrumentalists can play obbligatos with the choirs; accompany hymns sung by the congregation; accompany choirs, groups, or soloists; play preludes, postludes, and other service music; and perform many other helpful activities. Such accompaniment is limited only by imagination and by the availability of quality performers. One point to be remembered is that instrumentalists used in public service should be good. They can be used in any service, at any time an organ would be used. They can either play with the organ or as a substitute for it.

If a church orchestra is being organized, it is wise for two groups to be formed: one for beginners and one for more advanced players. Both groups are equally important but decidedly different in purpose (and sound). The senior group will perform at regular and special services in the ways already listed. The junior group will serve in children's meetings and the like and will primarily be a training ground for musicians who are or will be needed in the senior group. This organization implies two things: (1) The junior group should be used to a great extent for training people to play instruments that are needed or will be needed in the senior group, and (2) there should be a concentrated training program to teach junior group members to play and to play well. The task is not quite as great as it sounds, for most beginners will be young people who go to a school that has a band or orchestra as part of the elective courses offered; much of their training will thus be doubled, to everyone's advantage.

Other specialty groups may be formed as well—groups like a recorder choir, a handbell choir, or an accordian choir—but music for those groups is sparse in the finding and will quite often have to be arranged to suit the abilities and makeup of the individual group. Texture in music is almost wide open these days, and almost any combination from a tuba trio to a Cordovox quartet will be accepted.

Writing for groups made up of whatever is available is not really difficult if the arranger has the native talent. He should begin by writing everything in concert pitch (piano pitch) and then transposing as is necessary later. A string quartet, for example, can use SATB music or a piano part, and the only part that needs transposing is the viola part. The viola should play the tenor part, using the center line of the treble clef as middle C.

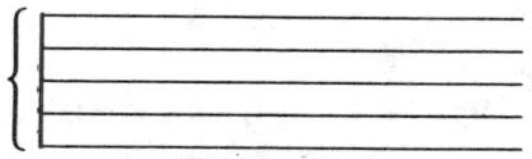

←Middle C

Treble Clef

For an instant arrangement, the SATB parts should be used for the instrumentalists and the accompanist's part for the pianist or organist.

Many churches do not have the instruments required for the balanced orchestration most published materials are written for, but the problem is not insoluble. Arrangements can be made for the instruments available. Any music not under copyright can be freely arranged. Thus a contrapuntal rendition of "Holy, Holy, Holy" for four kazoos and tub bass may sound ghastly, but it is legal. However, arranging music under copyright is a different matter. Copyright and renewal for a pre-1978 work can last for a total of seventy-five years. For a post-January 1, 1978, work, copyright lasts for the author's life plus fifty years; for post-January 1, 1978, works made for hire, and for post-January 1, 1978, anonymous and pseudonymous works (unless the author's identity is revealed in Copyright Office records), copyright lasts for seventy-five years from publication or one hundred years from creation, whichever is shorter. Music that is still under copyright cannot legally be arranged in any way without the permission of the copyright owner. If the arrangement is for use in the church and not for a paid performance or recording, most copyright owners will grant permission at a nominal fee or without charge, but permission must be secured from them if the work is under copyright. Further information on the International Copyright Laws can be obtained from the Copyright Office, The Library of Congress, Washington, D.C. 20559. These laws are international; so they apply in Canada and anywhere else, as is outlined in Copyright Office literature.

Leaders should be creative with sound. They should work on different combinations and different registrations. A trombone quartet can just use male quartet music, true, but it will sound better if it is taken up a third or so into a more mellow range. Similarly, a flute, oboe, or clarinet trio can use SSA music but will sound better if transposed up a bit, though here a fifth or so is better.

If the words to the music being played are known by the listeners, more "ministering" can sometimes be done. Using pieces whose words are known by the listeners is a good idea when using instrumental numbers for offertories and special numbers. People can then think on the words as the music is being played. Music that does not have well-known words is better used as a prelude or postlude, when people may prefer to meditate on a variety of thoughts individually. In any case, the selection should fit the mood of the service.

Leadership within the group

A final consideration is leadership, or executive groups, within the musical group. The number of members in a group's leadership body and the leaders' respective functions will vary from group to group. However, the following twelve titles and descriptions should fit the leadership body of any group. A large group should have a different person for each position. A smaller group should simply give multiple jobs to its fewer individuals.

1. President—chairs executive meetings; represents the group to the music committee, minister of music, and director; and serves as a public relations man for the group
2. Vice-President—recruits members and arranges group devotions
3. Librarian—sets out, collects, repairs, and files the group's music
4. Secretary/Membership Chairman—records attendance, takes minutes at executive meetings, follows-up absentees, and advises the treasurer of hospitalizations and so forth
5. Treasurer—collects the group members' offering or dues; counts, records, and banks that money; makes payment for group activities, cards, and rose bowls for hospitalized members, bereaved members, and members who have had babies; and provides a report of finances to the church treasurer at the end of the fiscal year
6. Social and Recreational Convenor—plans and administers social and recreational activities for the group, including activities, food, transportation and so on (this person may organize a committee to help with these duties)
7. Robe Custodian—fits, distributes, repairs, cleans, and stores the group's vestments
8. Properties Director—supplies, repairs, and places the stands, risers, and other equipment needed by the group
9. Section Leaders—have superior musical ability and Christian character; assist weaker performers in sectional

rehearsals, regular rehearsals, and such other times and ways as may be open to them

10. Nursery Coordinator—provides properly supervised child-care service for the children of the group members during rehearsals

11. Telephone Chairman—calls the other members of the group, personally or with the help of a committee, with messages that cannot be communicated at the regular rehearsal; the messages may be announcements of activities planned or canceled and emergency messages

12. Prayer-Partner Coordinator—encourages each member of the group to arrange for three people from the congregation who will pray for him as he ministers and to arrange for one person from the choir who will pray for him daily

5

Determining Appropriateness

This chapter deals with guidelines for selecting suitable, fit, proper, and relevant music for use in the church. Two approaches must be used: the pragmatic and the philosophical. It is not my intention to name specific songs to choose or avoid; rather, I want to provide assistance for every reader, of whatever denominational persuasion, in formulating criteria for determining the appropriateness of any piece of music, in any setting.

Questions Regarding the Music Itself

In a search for an answer to the question of appropriateness, it is most sensible to consider first those items that reflect on the practical aspects of the choice. The following questions and others like them are primary considerations regarding the music itself.

1. What group is going to sing the music, and what are the ages of the people in the group?
2. What are these peoples' sight-reading skills?
3. Is the music too difficult?
4. Is the music too trite?
5. Does the music have ranges beyond the group's capabilities?
6. Are there enough persons in the group for all the parts required by the music? (That is, does the music call for a

three-part men's chorus but will only two tenors be present the day the music is to be performed?)

7. Does the music have an excess of difficult chromaticism?

8. What is the level of ability of the accompanist(s) in view of what is written? Is the accompaniment too hard, too easy, or, perhaps, just plain bad?

9. Is there a degree of challenge to the music, yet not so much as to make it beyond the group's reasonable capabilities? Fresh and different things provide variety and challenges from the usual or from the trite. Variety in range, rhythm, melody, and harmony, as well as the best tool available to a choir—dynamic change—all contribute to the interest the group will have in doing the music.

10. What are the general aesthetic and musical levels of the persons who will perform the music and of the persons who will listen to it?

11. Does the music reinforce, support, and enhance the message; or does it detract from it, cheapen it, and obscure it?

12. In the desire to experiment with and expand on available resources—through the introduction of new styles, techniques, instrumentations, or electronics, for example—a basic question that Dr. Erik Routley posed in a 1975 lecture should not be forgotten: "Is it a *nice* noise?" His point was simple: Is a pleasant sound being produced? (It is assumed, of course, that a pleasant sound is what is wanted. Music about the death of Christ, for example, would perhaps be most effective if the sound was *not* pleasant.)

Questions Regarding the Words

There are also some basic, practical questions to be asked about the words.

1. Are the words scriptural? That is, are quotations from

the Bible correct and correctly used, and is the meaning of the text scripturally sound?

2. Are the words applicable both to the performers and to the persons who are expected to be listening to the text?
3. Is the text good literature? Is it profound, didactic, and accurate?
4. Is the text doctrinally sound; or does it hedge on important truth or introduce thoughts that are outside of sound biblical doctrine?
5. Are the words beautifully expressed?
6. Are the words meaningful to the average listener of today; or are they either too antiquated or too avant-garde to convey the desired message accurately?
7. Are the words appropriate for the age levels of singers and listeners alike?
8. Is the text appropriately wedded to the music? Are they saying the same thing?

Questions Regarding General Suitability

Finally, there are general questions of suitability.

1. Is the selection practical? Can it be done; and if so, does it serve the purpose at hand and move toward the objectives of the ministry?
2. Some music is better if it is done in expanded arrangements (orchestration and so forth). Other music is better if it is done simply. Does the way this music is to be done suit its content, style, and intended purpose?
3. Furthermore, is the music appropriate for the kind of performance being given? Some sacred music—both old and new—is written for the concert hall and is not suitable for use in the church's regular services. If it is to be service music, it must meet the needs of hearer and singer alike. If it is for a concert, then the piece needs a certain amount of entertainment value. If it is for a teaching ministry, it must have fitting content. Each of these kinds of music should be performed, but in appropriate settings.

4. Is the presentation of the best quality? A variety of styles, texts, and media should be used, but only one quality—the best. The quality of a presentation will determine its acceptance and consequent usefulness almost as much as will its style or the performance medium used.
5. Is the presentation an expression of many different ways of life, attitudes, and tastes? People have various ways of life, various attitudes, and various tastes; so any group of people is open to and needs various kinds of music. People do not so much know what they like as like what they know. The challenge, then, is to meet this variety of needs without causing offense to anyone. As much as is reasonable, each individual should be considered.
6. Has the decision of appropriateness been based on these pragmatic factors alone? The six following questions should also be considered.

Other Criteria

The preparation for any good music program involves much time spent in selecting the music to be used. Often the choice is made quite independently of any of the above guidelines: Often the choice is made solely on the basis of the leader's whim or taste, without consideration of either the practical or the philosophical aspects that should guide that choice. I believe that as responsible stewards of God's time, talents, and treasure, leaders ought to make their choices more carefully. The following listing of some abstract philosophical considerations is intended to help persons responsible for making choices to make them more carefully. These criteria should be applied to all the music done in the church—hymns, Sunday school choruses, the music of outside groups coming in, and so on—and not just to the choir's anthems or the "professional" music: Care must be taken, for singing is teaching.

1. Do the words, music, performance medium, and style *all* agree with the church's doctrinal position and philosophy of ministry?

2. Is the piece characterized by simplicity? Simplicity is not to be undervalued. Both grandeur and airiness can be uncluttered and simple. The spiral of "productions" without productivity should be avoided.

3. Does the piece reflect proper attitudes, and will performers and listeners be encouraged toward proper attitudes by it? There is no substitute for proper attitudes. Music, service, and even worship are all totally without benefit unless based on a proper attitude toward God, His Word, and His work in individual lives. Proper attitudes will be reflected in proper conduct and in a sensitivity to what is true, honorable, right, pure, lovely, of good reputation, excellent, and worthy of praise, as directed in Philippians 4:8.

4. Are the piece and its performance of high quality? Consideration of the above questions will assist in avoiding the trite, the lifeless, and the cheap. If music costs little or nothing in time, effort, concern, and money, it will also likely contribute little or nothing. Music that is thoughtless and careless will benefit no one. As Lovelace and Rice put it: "Today it is possible to find churches with a silver chalice for communion using paper-cup music for the liturgy."[1]

5. Does the piece fit the service, and does it serve its purpose properly? The power of music to enhance or create a mood or an effect must be recognized. The music must fit the service in which it is to be used. If the aim is worship, the music should be worshipful; if the aim is education, the music should be didactic. However, music must be used with discretion. It should guide, convict, encourage, comfort, exhort, challenge, teach, or do whatever other ministry is intended for it, but it must never coerce or capitalize on its emotional impact to the end that it becomes a manipulative tool. People should be moved to God through content, not through an emotional pitch.

6. Is the piece "non-food" music? Related to the matter of

---

[1]Austin C. Lovelace and William C. Rice, *Music and Worship in the Church* (Nashville: Abingdon, 1976), p. 99.

content is the subject of things to avoid. Non-food music—that which says very little of help—is to be avoided in much the same way as junk foods are to be avoided. Just as a balanced food diet is desirable, so a balanced musical diet is desirable.

Point six brings us to the question of what constitutes non-food music. It is said that rock music, for instance, has as one characteristic the use of simple repetitive phrases. The point is intended to be derogatory; yet often persons who tout it will direct or support the singing of a kyrie eleison or similar setting that is acceptable though equally repetitive. Other persons insist that it is the distinctive beat that separates rock music from the mainstream of musical offerings; yet many contemporary choral settings use the same beat in moderation in their accompaniments or as part of the choral score. Still other persons say that volume makes the distinction clear; yet the volume in 2 Chronicles 30:21 must have been tremendous.

No, the difference is not one of kind; it is one of degree. To give a definitive guideline of what is and what is not rock music is impossible. Several factors make such a definitive guideline impossible: for instance, a person's taste, background, age, level of musical education, and associational directives, as well as the volume level of the music, the accompaniment used, the place of performance, and the atmosphere at the performance are all contributing factors in each person's idea of whether a piece of music is rock music or not. Many people seek out an authority figure who has articulated their feelings and then rely on his reasoning to support their position. Charles Cleall and Bob Larson are opposed to the use of rock music by Christians; Gunnar Urang says that music is amoral and cannot be evil. "Experts" can be found to substantiate almost any position on almost any topic, but some conclusion must be reached here about the appropriateness of using rock music in the church. If nothing else, the integrity of the minister of music, the performers, and the church will be viewed in the light of their choices, which presumably are made in light of their purpose. Here is one basic question: What is my purpose? Why do I choose one style of music over another? Is it just taste, or do I have a series of reasons for my choice? It is hoped that there are reasons for decisions—reasoned thoughts like those outlined earlier in this chapter, for example.

It should be recognized that different is neither good nor bad, though the choice may be. Phil Kerr points out the truth that "all of the 'good old songs' were once *new songs*."[2] The old is not necessarily gold, and the new is not necessarily true either. Change need not be feared so much as complacency (in listeners and performers) or manipulation (by performers) should be. Complacency and manipulation are opposites, but each is destructive. At all times, the music used must reveal and reflect the truth.

If musical texts emphasize only the joy and comforts of modern Christianity without word of man's sinfulness, his need of a Savior, and Christ's atonement, they are not Christian; rather, they are humanistic. If music emphasizes an earthy beat, it is not going to communicate the holiness of a loving God. Trite texts fall far short of reaching the total man with the complete regeneration of God as revealed in His Word. The end does *not* justify the means. People are to be won to God by the ministry of His Spirit, who can use Scripture and people's accurate and sure word of testimony to convict people of the claims of Christ. In all that they do, the performers are to be holy, because God is holy, because they know that they were redeemed with the precious blood of Jesus—the spotless Lamb of God (1 Peter 1:14-19).

Christian performers are not called to use Madison Avenue, nor are they called to apathy. They are God's "workmanship, created in Christ Jesus for good works" (Eph. 2:10, NASB).

---

[2]Phil Kerr, *Music in Evangelism,* 4th ed. (Glendale, Calif.: Gospel Music Publishers, 1954), p. 65.

They should be careful not to smear the clarity of their calling by doing anything that is outside of the revealed character and nature of God. They should be careful not to offend the nature of God by the use of inappropriate music. Music that is sloppily done, in bad taste, or irrelevant is inexcusable in the Christian church. Certainly everyone makes mistakes, but no one needs to make all the mistakes. Christian musicians should learn from the character of God, as it is revealed in the Bible and in the person of Jesus Christ, and respond with music that fits, is proper and suitable, and is relevant for presenting Christian truths to the world around them.

The same sermon topic is not expected week after week, nor is the same subject matter or style in music wanted week after week. The "top ten" from the hymnal should not be belabored. Praise anthems should not be used continuously. All *appropriate* styles should be used; for although the needs and tastes of people vary, everyone should be confronted with the claims of Christ, which lead to salvation, training, and worshipful adoration of the worthy and holy God.

Because of the nature and power of music, it is a force that can be mightily used for good (see Exod. 15:20-21; 2 Sam. 6:14-15; 1 Chron. 16:5-6; 23:3-5; Psalms 149; 150; and so forth) or can be used as a display of the fallen state of man (Exod. 32:18-19; Judg. 21:21; 1 Sam. 30:16; Job 21:11; Psalm 69:12; Amos 5:23; 6:5). It is a medium of communication and expression in its own right, without a text. The Old Testament indicates that the abuse of it is not a new thing, nor is it to be viewed as a passing thing. Music that is befitting God must be jealously guarded and sacrificially prepared and performed. Neither old nor new is good or bad, but all should be judged on quality, truthfulness, musicianship, and the other criteria for determining whether or not it is appropriate. Everyone differs on the outside boundaries, but everyone should stand united on the central truths of what is best: that which God uses to speak to hearts about Himself and His truth: that which leads people to a vibrant, practical, and personal life in Christ.

Here again both the text and the music are of equal importance; there must be an appropriate marriage resulting in a unity of sound and message. Furthermore, it is impossible for all biblical truth to be expressed in every song; just as there is variety in Scripture, so there should be variety in the presentation of Scripture. An entire message can be adequately portrayed in several songs, and such coordination is desirable in most situations.

One final caution needs to be repeated. Leaders have a responsibility to evaluate quality of performance and accuracy of content, for both must be firmly upheld if an accurate portrait of Christ is to be drawn in the music. But to attribute motive to a performer is to judge, and that is wrong.

6

Rehearsals

Many directors have a knowledge of music and skills in conducting, but they still fail in rehearsal. The problem may be one of practice site, rehearsal time or duration, or the procedure followed. This chapter will, in some measure, deal with those topics and offer some techniques and hints for a more successful practice time.

Any director must know basic theory and the standard conducting patterns. Knowledge of both is assumed here and will not be dealt with further than to refer the leader to a listing of a few books on conducting that may prove helpful. This list is contained in the bibliography at the back of this book.

Place of Rehearsal

Main auditorium

As a rule, there are two choices for a practice location: the main auditorium (the sanctuary) or a robing room, often mistakenly referred to as the choir room. For the sake of illustration in this chapter, I shall assume that we are referring to a senior choir. The advantage of rehearsing in the main auditorium is that the group is in the position and setting in which it will perform. Thus the choir members hear the piano and organ that will be used on Sunday and they feel familiar with the surroundings. Also, the sound produced in rehearsal approximates the sound that will come in the service—with one devastating difference: when the seats are full of people, the clear, resonant sound goes and a deadness sets in which can take the group by surprise. A result of this difference in sound is often a good rehearsal followed by a poor performance; because the singers cannot hear anyone else singing, they become hesitant themselves, usually subconsciously. Another disadvantage of using the main sanctuary for choir practices is that the entire room must be heated or cooled for the use of relatively few individuals. At today's costs for energy, temperature control for rehearsals is expensive. Not to have it is just as bad, though, because it forces singers to use their voices for extended periods of time under poor conditions. There must be adequate air flow, lighting, and temperature control.

Robing room

Many churches have faithfully installed what they call a choir room. This room is used for gown storage, as an assembly room, as a music library and sorting room, as the director's office, and as a general practice room (sometimes all at once!). The room is invariably too small; has too low a ceiling; is not separately heated, ventilated, and cooled; and is generally unsatisfactory. To have a room is not enough. It must be the *right* room. Thus a third choice for a rehearsal room is needed, but it is a choice that is not really a choice at all; rather, it is an imperative for optimum performance. A proper rehearsal room is needed.

Rehearsal room

To begin with, a rehearsal room is expensive. It costs a good deal of money to build and equip a rehearsal room properly, but the cost is a fraction of the cost of a gymnasium. A rehearsal room will yield much more return in the public ministry, partly because on the average a third of any given service is music, but not much of the service is physical education. If such a practice room is built as an addition to an existing building or as a part of a new one, several things should be considered. First, regarding its location, the room should be easily accessible to the main auditorium and on the same level as the auditorium, but the two places should not be so close that a full rehearsal in progress can be heard in the sanctuary. It is also advantageous for the rehearsal room to be near the nursery. The remaining factors concern the properties of the room itself.

1. Its acoustics should be as nearly as is possible the same as those of the main auditorium when full. An acoustical engineering firm can take care of this matter.
2. It should have independently controlled heating, cooling, and ventilation.
3. Its ceilings should be a minimum of 12 feet high, with even lighting at a minimum of 45 footcandles at normal reading level. There should be a minimum of 10 square feet of floor space per person, based on the maximum number of people that could possibly fit into the regular choir loft. In addition to this space, 20 square feet should be allowed for each instrumentalist who may accompany the group, for each instrumentalist in the church orchestra, and for the director. To determine the size of the room, therefore, one would need to know the maximum capacity of the choir loft (75, for example) and the maximum number of members of the orchestra (25, for example). For the choir the room would have to be 75 x 10 square feet + 60 square feet (pianist, organist, and director)=810 square feet, plus space is needed for any orchestral accompaniment that may be used from time to time, usually not more than 12 persons; so 12 x 20=240 square feet. Thus the total size of 1,050 square feet is required to match the other facilities of this building (the orchestra would easily fit into this same space).
4. The room should be bright, cheerful, and tastefully decorated—not hospital white with a gray rug!
5. It should adjoin the following rooms:

    A. The minister of music's office.
    B. An office to be shared by the other directors.

C. Men's and ladies' washrooms with full length mirrors.

D. The music library, with a sorting table.

E. Ventilated robe-storage rooms for gowns and costuming for all groups.

6. It should contain the following equipment:

A. An adequate organ and piano.

B. Portable risers (all portable equipment must in fact be portable—that is, that it must go through the doors, it must be easily transported, and so forth), unless permanent risers are preferred.

C. A blackboard (with painted staffs) behind the director, in a position easily seen by all the group.

D. A good quality tape recorder, turntable, amplifier, and speakers to use for recording and playing back the group's music and for playing other recorded music. There would ideally be both a cassette and a reel-to-reel tape machine; for soundtracks come in the superior reel form, while normal recording is more easily done on a cassette machine.

E. Recording jacks to the main sound room of the church for full-track recording.

7. The choir room should be scheduled for use by all choirs, ensembles, bands, or orchestras in the church program. Thus the sanctuary is kept free for other uses and all the noise is in one place. The rehearsal room should also be scheduled for drama rehearsals, for workshops, classes, seminars, and meetings, and for any other use compatible with the music department, which has first priority in scheduling the room.

The advantages of such a room are multiple: it is not necessary to transport music; the sound is the same as that which will be experienced in actual performance; it is cheaper to heat and cool than the larger sanctuary (which is then freed for other uses should the need arise); music, robes, supplies, files, and so forth are readily accessible to the choir and its director;

the room serves a multiple function; and so on. To a moving, vital program, the addition of such a room is a distinct advantage.

Time and Duration of Rehearsal

The next question to be addressed is that of when rehearsal should take place. This will be determined largely by two factors. One is the general policy and philosophy of the church; the other is dependent on what is expected from the group or the department as a whole. If the church has as an objective having all the regular church activities on one weeknight, two possibilities arise. The first possibility is holding a necessarily short practice as one of the activities scheduled consecutively for that one evening. The second possibility is the scheduling of programs that run concurrently; people would then choose one activity over another, because they would be barred from being in both by reason of the scheduling. The second factor to be considered in determining when rehearsal should be held—that of the expectations of the group or program—must also be introduced here before all these points are discussed further. A mediocre or an excellent program will take correspondingly different amounts of time, assuming average musicians in both situations. Let us use the senior choir once again as an example. If a decent job is to be done on a call to worship and an anthem or two, plus work on two or three concerts or cantatas per year, a minimum of two to two and a half hours' rehearsal time is probably required each week.

The picking and choosing may now begin. If the church wishes all activities to be held in succession on one evening, with a midweek service of an hour to an hour and a quarter's duration, then a good quality choir is almost automatically rendered impossible. For example, if the service begins at 7:30 P.M., as most do, and runs to 8:30 or 8:45, as most do, then it is logical that the choir cannot begin before 8:45 or 9:00. A minimum two-hour practice session then runs to about 11:00 P.M., making a very late night for people who have already worked a full day and for their children, who are in the nursery or child-care facility.

The other alternative for a one-night system is to run the midweek service and choir practice simultaneously. This choice is usually unacceptable, because it forces people out of Bible study and prayer in order to sing in the choir, and vice versa.

There must be a decision, therefore, as to the quality of program desired for the senior choir's ministry. If mediocre is good enough, then an hour and a quarter will do for rehearsal. On the other hand, if the best reasonable offering to God is what is wanted (and few people could argue otherwise), adequate time for rehearsal must be provided.

The obvious disadvantage of holding practice and other activities on various nights is that families soon start running Mom to church Monday for the mission circle, Dad and Sue on Tuesday for a committee meeting and youth group, the whole family on Wednesday for Bible study and prayer, Mom and Dad Thursday for choir, Johnny on Friday for boys' club, Sue again on Saturday for a youth group social, and everyone back all day Sunday again. My example may seem farfetched, but in many homes it at least seems that this is the way it is some weeks. Obviously not all of these activities are scheduled every week; as a matter of fact, at the most five of them are, so the problem is somewhat lessened already. Sunday and Wednesday (or whatever) will not change. They are regular, traditional, and beneficial services. Thus the clubs, youth groups, and choir are left to be tended to.

In a very large church, the clubs or groups could conceivably be run at the same time as when the choir practices, automatically eliminating people from serving in more than one activity that night. However, it is hoped that the number of people who would have to choose one activity over another would be quite small.

Now we have:

Sunday—two services and Sunday school

Monday—boys' and girls' clubs
Tuesday—women's club, men's club, board meeting, and committee meeting as needed (usually once a month each, taking care of all four Tuesdays in the month)
Wednesday—Bible study and prayer
Thursday—youth groups and senior choir
Friday—socials (Saturday night socials make too many people too sleepy on Sunday morning)
Saturday—free

We have succeeded in freeing one day at least. But what about the youth choir? And the junior choir? And the primary choir? Then, of course, there are the church orchestra, the chancel choir, and the many ensembles and soloists who have to rehearse. Plus, the Christian education workers' training meetings, and the evangelism and discipleship classes, along with the membership or baptismal class must not be left out. It is obvious that everything cannot be scheduled and any major time slot still be left open. The larger a church is, the more diversified are its ministries and its responsibilities. People must be provided with an avenue for service in keeping with their gifts, talents, and abilities. There will be duplication of leadership, membership, and scheduling—that is just a fact—if a full and vibrant church program is in operation.

What remains to be done, then, is to set the church's priorities. The most important decision to be made must be made by the staff and the church board, which includes representatives of all groups. These people may not be personally involved in everything, but they will, it is hoped, be aware of everything and be concerned about everything. The scheduling should be done in such a way as to secure the maximum value from each ministry offered. As much as is reasonably possible, the needs, purpose, and value of each group should be analyzed, an equitable schedule drafted, and people granted the right to choose which activities they want to be involved in. On the basis of impact, service, public ministry, and time in the services themselves, music emerges as a high priority. Adequate rehearsal time simply must be provided to ensure a growing, quality program with growing, quality groups made up of growing, quality individuals, and having rehearsals on a separate night seems to be the only way to do that.

Procedure for Rehearsal

After a rehearsal time has been scheduled, the question of what should be done during the time allotted arises. (We shall continue to use the senior choir as an example.)

Director's preparation

For the director, much of the work is done long before he steps up to the choir. His background work includes, among other things:

1. Recruiting members. Although this is included in the job definition of the president of the choir, the director should still make it his concern.
2. Selecting his music: anthems, service music, and pieces to be used for concerts, special programs, and practice (sight-singing and so forth).
3. Matching the music with performance dates, while paying particular attention to special events for which music must be ordered and for which longer rehearsal times will be needed. The director should plan at least three months ahead for regular music and six months ahead for special music. (Planning for a full year is advised. It makes less pressure for the director and allows the group members to plan other activities around a posted schedule of engagements.)
4. Reserving the rehearsal room for the day and time required.
5. Making sure that the instruments are there and in good repair and tune. Chairs, music folders, and so on are all his responsibility, though he may have a librarian, properties director, and other people actually performing the tasks. Chalk, pencils, and other supplies should also be checked.

6. Assuring that sufficient budget funds are available to carry the group through the year.
7. Publicizing the group to the church, both for continued support and for the possibility of adding members.
8. Drawing up a rehearsal plan. It should include things like identification of the piece to be rehearsed, things to note or watch for in it, time to be spent on it, aim in doing it, performance date, file number (for location of music in storage), and preparation of the devotional time (if he is to lead it).
9. Knowing his music well before beginning. The director and his choir do not "learn together." That phrase is nice and humble sounding; but the director is there to lead, not to be the blind leading the blind.
10. Getting the music to the accompanists ahead of rehearsal, if they so desire or if he feels that the practice would go more smoothly if they ran over it beforehand. Generally at least a week ahead is required; and it makes no difference to the director, because he is at least two months ahead in his planning. He should go over the music with them to establish tempos and so on.
11. Planning a devotional time. This task is in the job responsibilities of the vice-president; but it should be verified by the director, who may choose to lead it or to delegate it to the vice-president.
12. Setting up the system of music distribution and collection. Once again, a librarian should do the task, but it will be administered by the conductor. Having all the music to be practiced in folders is perhaps the quickest and easiest method.
13. Marking all the music before rehearsal to save time later.
14. Planning growth for the group and for individual members. He should think of ways to stretch their abilities and sights, in their music and in their lives.
15. Planning to provide a distinctively Christian atmos-

phere, attitude, and format to the rehearsal time. It is a time for honoring God and preparing well to minister in His name. He should plan an exciting first rehearsal particularly. Everyone at rehearsal should enjoy himself: rehearsing should be enjoyable work.

Rehearsal procedure

With this preparation done, what then are some general guidelines for the procedure of the rehearsal?

1. It should be begun and ended on time! The director should contract together with the group that if they will arrive on time, he will quit on time.
2. The director should work at promoting and developing proper spiritual and musical attitudes. This can largely be done through the opening time of devotions. If he is the minister of music, he should *minister* to them.
3. The director should follow his rehearsal plan, though flexibility is critical.
4. The director should seat people in their proper order according to the seating plan.
5. The director should develop keener listening habits in members. He should have them listen for blend, balance, pitch, intonation, rhythmic unity, and phrasing. He should also have them listen to each other to develop a sense of refinement, sensitivity, and unity in sound.
6. One way of aiding listening is for the director to have the choir members do some sight-singing without the accompaniment. The members will be forced to sing out, and there will be no instrumental "cover" for them to hide behind.
7. The director should be explicit in giving instructions. He should let the members know not only what he wants, but why he wants it.
8. The director should use humor. "People do not have time to waste" is true, but "People need to laugh" is also true.

9. The director should build on strengths and nurture confidence. Superior performance will follow.
10. If the director is new and the group is established, the director should "make haste slowly." He should not try to change in one week the way everything has been done. He should build on the good points and strengthen weak ones as necessary, but with sensitivity and purpose.
11. The director should instruct his choir members in the policy that any additional markings on the music should be added by all members to all parts. The next time the piece is sung, the music will undoubtedly be shifted around; and if only the altos mark a change in the alto part, next time they will each get a soprano's copy for sure!

HINTS FOR TEACHING

The common thinking today is that it is impossible for a person to sing and be heard without a microphone; and the bulk of the music aired today is not providing a good model for people in this respect. Concert singers, or even persons with beautifully clear and natural voices, can seldom be heard. Oliver Mogck, of Bethel College, St. Paul, Minnesota, once said that "you must learn to sing as though the microphone had never been invented." "That is," he added later, "you must learn to sing 'with proper projection and sufficient energy.' "

The vocal cords are like the biceps: they are muscles, and a person either uses them or loses them. Just like any other muscle, they can get flabby and lazy if not exercised. A smooth, extended range is nothing more than the result of doing vocal push-ups. Clear, clean, pure tone through as wide a range as is possible is the ideal. If it is not easy, it is not right. Singing is not difficult if done properly; rather, it is a delight and a pleasure.

Good singing can be assisted by the conducting, and it often begins there. Conducting is not beating time. It is the act of interpreting the music so that it comes alive and does not remain ink, paper, and sound. The director should conduct like an artist, like an interpreter. Directing is more than flailing one's arms: it is sensitivity and strength communicated through the eyes, the facial expression, the hands, the breath, and the size and shape of the conducting pattern.

The director should approach the music as a whole: he should watch for flow. He should not be ruthlessly tied to the written tempos, speed variations, volumes, and so forth; rather, he should interpret in an appropriate way what the piece is saying. He should maintain the rhythm certainly, if the piece demands it (in a march, for example), and he should not get "gooey" with the music either. Maintaining rhythm will also help the group to maintain concentration and pitch, but the director should remember that sensitivity to the message should be the overriding factor in his approach to the music.

Bearing these things in mind, the director should begin teaching his choir with the aid of suggestions like these:

1. The director should refine his communications with the choir members as they are singing. Using *ss* instead of *sh* quiets them more quickly, simply because it is easier to hear.
2. When the music warrants it, the director should shape the phrases with volume variations—like this: . Long notes, especially at the end of phrases, may be held freely as the volume rises, or falls, or rises and then falls.
3. The director should have the choir members end all words together, not just the words that conclude with a consonant.
4. The director should work at having the group always bring out the short note in a mixed passage. All too often the short note is neglected, leaving a dip in the musical phrase.
5. In many mixed passages there are dotted notes. Often they are really suspensions. The director should not allow the sound to drop off on them.
6. The director should keep diction as natural sounding as possible.[1] *Father* is *father,* not *fawthah*. He should be alert,

[1]See Madeleine Marshall, *The Singer's Manual of English Diction* (New York: Schirmer, 1953).

though, to more efficient ways of getting this natural sound. *I,* for example, is bad for long notes if it is sung in the middle of the mouth. If, however, it is made a diphthong and pronounced as *a͡h-ee,* the pronunciation stays natural but the sound is improved.

7. The director should watch for points of expression and interpretation and use them as the meaning and style of the piece demand, keeping in mind the basic law that the music should *do* what the text *says*.

8. Much of the difficulty encountered by any director results from a lack of concentrated effort toward awareness on the part of the choir or group. It is expedient for conductors to do all they can to make the music living and interesting. For example, when the choir members sing the Savior's name, Jesus, it ought to be something special—Jesus. They should think of who He is, and what He has done! Concentration on both technique and meaning is vital to the ultimate impact of a piece of music.

9. Anything a director does to simplify and clarify things for his choir members is not only appreciated by them but is also an effective way of teaching. For example, most conductors have no difficulty with the Italian terms used in music. But most amateur choir members ignore them, probably largely because they do not know what the terms mean. Instead of explaining these terms in depth, the director should try to make ''visualized'' definitions for them. A three-four piece at one beat to the bar could be pictured as skating. A moderate four-four piece with eighth-note rhythm could be pictured as a drum major strutting in front of his band. This kind of teaching will help to bring the standard terms into a new light of meaning for the choir members.

PROBLEMS TO BE DEALT WITH

How do I know who is going to show up to sing in the

summer? Will I have enough singers, in the right balance, to do the anthem I planned on doing? Those are common questions, but ones that are needlessly asked over and over again without something being done about getting answers. The director should think about trying this, though: He should draw up a vacation chart and post it in the rehearsal room. On it should be listed all practices and performances scheduled for the entire summer. The names of all choir members, accompanists, and so forth should be placed on the chart; then each person named should fill in his vacation time. Any late additions to the practice and performance schedule should be made at least a week ahead of time and noted in a different color. Most folk know a week ahead if they are going to take off for the weekend, and most know their holiday schedules at the beginning of the summer. In this way, the conductor knows at least a week in advance if the anthem will need to be changed. Some people will still decide at the last minute to go away, but there will be less of an unknown factor than if no chart is used and the director has to wonder about all of the members. Using such a chart does mean that an extra piece must be nearly ready to perform so that it can be substituted, but the way to be prepared is by beginning to practice each piece four to five weeks ahead of its scheduled date of performance. Just running through it a time or two for a few weeks brings familiarity and takes away the last minute pressure of learning and polishing an anthem at one sitting, a boring experience and a near impossibility. People who work shifts will also benefit from this system. Even if they must miss every second rehearsal, they will still have practiced the piece at least twice.

At long last the director has made all possible preparations for a successful rehearsal, and then a new tenor comes. The director should rejoice! But the new tenor cannot sing! And he does it loudly! What should the director do? He should audition the new man (see pages 59-62) just as he has auditioned everyone else. Simply showing up at a church board meeting or Sunday school teachers' meeting does not get one onto the board or permit him to teach, and neither should just showing up be the criterion for getting into the choir. Believers have a responsibility to make the best sound they can in honor of God. Just because the sound is to be joyful does not mean that that is *all* it is to be.

Many problem voices can be helped if the director has the time and qualifications to do so (if not, he should recommend private instruction). One thing he will want to do to be able to help persons with problem voices is to study as many of the fine books on vocal technique and production that are listed in the bibliography as he can. From those books he can gain insights both into problems associated with singing and into their solutions. A second thing he will want to do to help problem singers is to remember that *everyone* thinks he sings the right way. No one assumes that he would ever do something wrong all his life. Thus, any changes suggested should be said with care, sensitivity, accuracy, and an attitude of wanting to help make singing easier and more beautiful. The director should remember also this key in vocal work: if the sound does not come easy, it is wrong, either in range or in formation.

Following are some of the more common voice problems and some exercises that may help to alleviate them. I am once again indebted to Oliver Mogck for his guidance.

1. Tight throat—trying to get a loud, "operatic" sound by squeezing it out. The singer must *feel* what his throat is like when it is loose in order to be able to recognize the difference. An exercise like singing a moderately low *hung-ung-ung-ung* will likely help. The back of the tongue and the palate must be loose and open. The person should be told that any imitation of sound is bad; each individual's voice must be natural.
2. Whiteness (sometimes called oralization)—lots of teeth and a skinny sound, caused by opening the mouth horizontally () instead of vertically (). (By the way, this problem is simply and beautifully illustrated by holding a

rubber band and stretching it first the wrong way, horizontally, and then the right way, vertically. Any visualization will assist learning). Like tight throat, whiteness is also a tightness problem, only this time the tightness is more at the front of the mouth than at the back. The solution is the same: *hung-ung-ung-ung*. The idea again is for the singer to feel a natural looseness. When whiteness is a problem, there is little or no resonance above the roof of the mouth, causing a pinched sound. Instead, the nasal-pharynx area should be open; for vowels must exist in space, and they need the resonance of the nasal-pharynx area for a full sound.

3. Nasality—the opposite problem to whiteness. Alleviation of this problem is begun by having the singer "open up" everything in his head, as a conscious act. Then he should "feel" the sound move around as the director helps him place it in the nasal passages and then down through all the resonance areas to the chest. *Hung-ung-ung-ung* should be used again. *Hung-aah,* which will give a greater feel of the open sound once placement is achieved and tightness is relaxed, should also be used.

4. Vowel shallowness—caused by jaw tension. The singer should let his jaw "fall off" while singing *blah-blah* on a five-note ascending and descending scale. Having him sing *hm* on the same scale with teeth touching and then without will point out again the difference in sound and feel between a closed and a relaxed sound. To avoid jaw tension, he should sing at a very easy, relaxed level—he should not push. Part of the cause of vowel shallowness is children's trying to sing like adults. One should recognize the natural age-level characteristics of the voice and not go against them.

5. Shallow breathing—has two major causes: one is trying to sing with only enough air for talking; the other is incorrect posture. A person does not sing just with his voice box—he must sing with all his mind, body, and soul, all of which must be restfully alert. Just as a person's arm immediately responds to an object thrown at him, so a per-

son's body, mind, and spirit must respond in singing: they must be totally relaxed until needed, and then they must do what comes naturally: they must combine to help the person sing with alertness and calmness. For work in breath control, singers should sing *hm-hm-hm-hm-ah-ah-ah-ah-ah*, holding the fermata as long as a full sound can possibly be maintained; then they should breathe quickly and sing an ascending and descending five-note scale twice, ending again with a fermata. One long hold is not too difficult to manage, but the second one will point out the importance of that snatch breath in between. Donald Hustad is known for saying "See the conductor? He's right over the top of your music, isn't he?" The point is simply that when a person is sitting straight, the angle of his head will keep his throat at the optimum angle and will help him to concentrate on both the music and the director. Good posture, respiration, and resonance (via placement and relaxation) will yield good tone production, a basic in good singing. Finally, all sound must have good diaphramatic support to be controlled properly. It is of critical importance that the singer be completely loose and free inside the chest, throat, and mouth to sing well.

6. There are many other problems, such as improper diction, improper phrasing, and so on, but they are often dealt with by correcting the first five problems and then adding a concentrated serving of common sense. Extending a limited range, overcoming use of the head voice, correcting soft singing, and dealing with voice color variation are all more technical studies and will not be discussed here. The reader is encouraged to consult some of the fine books listed in the bibliography.

TWO FINAL NOTES

Two final notes on rehearsal discipline: 1. It is true that strict training in exacting the beauty and meaning of a piece will yield rich dividends in the final sound of the performance;

but what is more important is that the piece will have more meaning for those who sing it and for those who will hear it as a finished work. 2. Discipline mixes very nicely with concern and humor to make a good rehearsal technique.

7

Special Productions

In this chapter we shall look at many things that are involved in putting on special productions, including cantatas, oratorios, musicals, tours, concerts, recitals, or anything similar. Consideration will be given to the questions of whether or not a church should spend time on special productions, exactly what kind of production should be done, how it can be different from every other production in town, who should do it, and where. But the first decision to be made is whether or not even to bother doing anything outside the bounds of the weekly service ministry.

VALIDITY

Any special program could take a lot of time, effort, and money. Music must be bought. Costuming, lighting, and promotional materials, should they be used, must be paid for. Operators for the sound system, lights, and special effects may need to be found and trained. Extended practice sessions will likely be needed, not to mention all the planning and organizational time that will be necessary on the part of the director and his assistants. On the other hand are the possibility of a great outreach for Christ into the community, the provision of some top-quality Christian entertainment in the church, plus the specific goals of the production itself, be they evangelism, mission emphasis, discipleship, worship, challenge to stewardship, or whatever. The decision to have a special production or not can only be made after all the facts have been considered and judged according to their relative significance.

Most churches and directors will already have some idea of whether or not they are in favor of such activities, and most of them of course are favorable. Most churches and directors will also already have some idea of whether or not the special production should be a play, a cantata, or a concert. It is surprising that many people regard one form of the arts as sacred and another as secular. Many people will accept a cantata but would shy away from the use of drama, painting, dramatic readings, and other valid forms of expression. It is not the intent of this work to debate the relative merits of each form of expression; rather, it is simply to point out that perhaps this whole area needs to be rethought and a uniform system of belief in the use of the arts constructed.

To help people make sound decisions about whether to put on a special production or not, the following illustration and list are provided. Since most senior choirs do cantatas, let us use the production of a cantata for our illustration. The cantata king of North America is probably John W. Peterson. His works are usually about three-quarters of an hour in length and will likely take about fifteen to twenty times that amount of time for rehearsals—about twelve to fifteen hours, assuming a moderately good choir. To that time must be added the preparatory time of the director and the accompanists and the time to be donated by persons who will be responsible for any other extras needed. (These amounts of time will vary from church to church and from performance to performance.) If spotlights will be used for the soloists, narrators, and so forth, someone will need to run them. If the program is on other than a regular church-service night, ushers will be required. Should the sound system in the church not be of sufficient quality or versatility, someone will be needed to operate a new rented system; in any case a sound technician will be necessary, as a rule. When the time it takes to print and distribute advertising and programs has been added, then the amount of time that will be involved can be estimated. This estimate of time should then be multiplied by a least one and one-half to make up for human error (and the more humans the more error) and for things that people forgot to consider. So that is *who* is needed and what the cost in hours will be, but how about *what* is needed and how much it will cost? Here is a suggested beginning list of items to be considered:

1. Music
2. Costuming—things like tuxedo rental for the director if it is to be a formal, evening concert; and corsages for the accompanists are a nice way of expressing appreciation for all their extra hours of work
3. Special lighting effects—rheostats to dim lights in various parts of the building; one or two spotlights for soloists, narrators, and so forth; and other items, depending on the kind of production
4. Sound-system additions if they are required—such things as wireless microphones are very freeing and effective, but they require additional receivers and set up time, as well as the rental cost of the microphones themselves
5. Supplies for advertising—posters, fliers, bulletin inserts, and programs for the night of the concert are all to be considered here
6. Hall rental—if the church building is not to be used
7. Additional janitorial fees—possibly not needed if the church is used, but something that should be checked if the program is to be held on a night other than a normal service night
8. Additional salaries—for the director if he is only part-time and will be putting in extra hours; for secretarial time; for technicians to run the lights or sound; and so on
9. Local radio and television time—if the program is good enough, it may be aired on local radio or television; this, too, will likely cost, though some cable stations do provide free time for community programming

10. Orchestrations or taped backgrounds
11. Other miscellaneous items—coffee and doughnuts for the choir for the last rehearsal or two, out of appreciation for their hard work; a live recording of the program for pressing into a commemorative record later; and so forth

All those things cost money. Many will be necessary, depending on the type of production; many may never be necessary at all. Of course, the main determining factor in all of this is: How far do I want to go? Much can be accomplished by the simple singing through of the work; and the complexity of the evening will be regulated by the nature of the church, the size of the budget, the imagination of the director, and the style of the music being performed. It is unwise to try to make a fancy concert out of simple, plain pieces. They will lose their impact in all the clutter of show that is going on. The key here is an offshoot of the chapter on appropriateness: Does it fit? Is it tasteful? Is it in keeping with the character and nature of the particular local church? All those things must be kept in mind. The message must be aided by the additional happenings, not totally obliterated by the pizzazz of the work of an overzealous, would-be producer with a tinsel strand where his good taste and common sense should be.

The kind of production that is chosen will vary from church to church and within a given church. Different media should be explored to determine which can be used, which will be most effective in communicating the message, and which will be the most accurate reflection of the church and of our Lord. In addition, care should be taken to recognize the nature of the members of the anticipated audience. Their socioeconomic status, degree of musical education, and degree of general background knowledge, along with their degree of conservatism, their ages, and the area in the country must all be taken into account. In order for any special work to be as effective as possible, the optimum number of factors in favor of its success should be employed. If a director finds himself in a large metropolitan city and in a church composed mainly of persons from the upper-middle class, several of whom are season-ticket holders to the ballet, symphony, or opera, he would be wise to select a different medium of expression than would be chosen for a small suburban church, just outside an industrial district, whose congregation is largely made up of blue-collar workers who thrive on country music. Once again, the guidelines for appropriateness come into play here. If the music does not fit within the guidelines established by the church, it should not be used.

One concluding point on deciding validity: Doing an activity solely as bait to get people into an evangelistic meeting or anything else is wrong and dishonest. Surely the claims of Christ can bear to be presented openly, with thanksgiving and joy, and need not be sneaked in on false pretenses. If part of the program is to include a brief message or testimony, a statement of that fact should be put right in the program and on the posters. I do not wish to exclude the presentation of the claims of Christ, but all things should be done properly and in order.

Kinds of Programs

Several things can be done in order to get variety in the special events of a church. Those considerations given above (pages 121-22) about appropriateness are important in making decisions about what should be done. In addition to those guidelines are the limits only of good taste and the director's imagination and resources. Many multimedia presentations are being used these days, more in the theater than in the church. They are usually high-powered audiovisual presentations that tend to bombard the senses. If what is to be portrayed is of sufficient dramatic impact and significance, such a medium may be used to advantage. But, generally speaking, the effort and great expense involved will not be warranted. It must be borne in mind that the money used to fund the activities of the church is given as a gift to God, not to the choir directors. If the uses of funds are not in keeping with good stewardship of the Lord's money and the Lord's people, the uses cease to become justifiable pursuits. Simpler and less expensive things can be done to enhance the impact of the message, which really is the aim after all.

Very little is as effective in adding to the overall impact of any mood created in music as good lighting is. A rheostat to dim the stage lights or multiple rheostats to use with various colors can be used to create subtle visual changes that will hardly be noticed by those observing but will communicate together with the words and music the changing mood or emphasis of the piece. Spotlights on the soloists or narrators will draw attention to them, emphasizing what they are saying and taking the audience's attention off the members of the main group so that they can change music, change their positions in the group, be seated, stand, or perform any other necessary movement that would otherwise prove distracting.

Costuming and small stage actions are a little more involved and usually a little more difficult to do. Many churches do not have a stage area big enough to hold the choir and its accompanists and leave much room for stage action. Costuming and stage actions need not be elaborate and complicated though, particularly if they are used in conjunction with lighting, because then no backdrops are needed. For instance, if there is a solo for an angel, a man (and I recommend a man) can be dressed in a white robe, if that suits the age of the piece; by contrast, if the angel appears in a contemporary musical, he can be dressed in white slacks and a white shirt: the effect will be the same. Similarly, after a clause such as, "And the shepherds said one to another," a half dozen "shepherds" sing the next section, in costume, from the side of the stage so that the spotlights will not show the other people in the background, who would be distractingly out of character.

In addition, leaders should consider making use of various instruments for accompaniment. One section accompanied by harp or string quartet will provide nice variety, with really very little effort. There is also the dramatic simplicity of a well done acappella section in contrast to the body of the number, which likely has rather full accompaniment. A special program called "Living Hymns" could be presented. It would include enactments of the stories behind many of the more well known hymns and congregational singing of these hymns. I can just about guarantee that there would be a fresh appreciation for the meanings of those hymns that would be hard to achieve in any other way. One thing that is certain is the value of such programs for those who are directly involved. There will come a sense of ministry, unity, achievement, and thankfulness that pays well for the many hours of work put into such programs.

Several other kinds of things can be done with musicians within the church. The members of a youth choir that is doing fairly well may be able to book some time at a recording studio in order to tour it and learn a little of what is involved in that end of music today, and in order to sing a bit, with the results put on reduplicated cassettes for their own use as "just a recording gig we did once." The pride and excitement those young people would feel is easy to imagine. Similarly, children's (or any other) choirs could tour instrument manufacturing or repair firms, music printers, or the civic concert hall; listen to a rehearsal of a symphony orchestra; and on and on. Such activities will broaden the horizons of those involved, let the world out there know that there are Christian music groups whose members are aware of what is happening in the world of music outside their own sphere, and may just result in opportunities to witness or encourage.

Also, styles and periods can be mixed today like never before. Leaders should not be afraid to include a wide range of music in any given program, unless the program is intentionally designed otherwise. Likewise, if a church has the abilities and time, there is nothing to prohibit its members from writing their own musical special.

In concluding this section, I encourage each director to be sure to check all the details for a performance twice as often as should be necessary, and then plan on mistakes—the perfect performance does not exist. He should give everyone involved a written assignment that states exactly what the purpose of the entire production is, what the person's specific part in it is, and whatever timetables are necessary. When the performance is finished, the director should thank everyone who helped in any way; then he should clean up and put back the borrowed or rented equipment.

Performances Outside the Group's Own Church

After much effort has gone into planning and executing a good musical evening, the question arises whether the group should schedule one or more performances outside its own church, thus using the result of all its work on more than just the one occasion. The answer will be determined in part by the flexibility of the group and the policy of the church; but generally an extended ministry is encouraged, as long as it does not interfere with the regular functions of the church. In other words, it is best if outside performances are not scheduled for a time when the people involved should be doing something at their own church, unless they go with the blessing of the senior minister and the church board. A person's primary Christian service is to the local church, and from there to the world.

Several questions should be considered before a group embarks on an outside engagement. They are:

1. Who should go?
2. Why are they going?
3. Is this group the best representative of this church and of Christ that could go? If not, should someone else go, or should no one go? People will very likely not be too impressed by a poor quality group, even if its members are doing their best. If the group's best is not very good, it should not travel around singing. Persons outside the group's own church may not appreciate what the group has to say because they will be concerned for the poor way it is being said. Their unexpressed thought may be, *My Johnnie's group could certainly do better than that.*

4. What attitudes will outside engagements encourage in those who go? A steady diet of teaching from the home church is invaluable; so care must be taken that feelings of wanderlust are not introduced in the group members, particularly in the youth.
5. Does the engagement have proper approval? Groups should go out as representatives of the church, and they should go only with the approval of the board and the ministers.
6. Can the engagement be made to coincide with the pastor's speaking engagement at another church? Many times a pastor will accept an invitation to speak at another local church. Such an engagement is often a good time for a group to go with him in support of his ministry. The program, its emphasis, and the like can be worked out ahead of time, and the evening can be put together as a unified package.
7. Where should the group go? Should it go to another church, a shopping center, a park, a nursing home of one variety or another, a camp, a picnic, a back-yard club, a vacation Bible school session, an airport, a bus depot, a train station—where? The group could go to any or all of those places, depending on the group's purpose and the willingness of its members to do a lot of work for seemingly little response.
8. Will enough persons be able to go so that the group can do a good job?
9. If the group is going out as an outreach ministry, are the members trained in evangelism and witnessing?
10. Will any other groups be present? If so, should association with their music or doctrinal stand be discouraged?
11. Is the place for the performance big enough to hold the group? On the other hand, is the group big enough to fill the place?
12. Will a portable public-address system be needed? If so, does the group, the church, or the place being visited have

one, or will one have to be rented? Who will run it, and who will pay for it? Is there electricity there for it? If so, how far away is the outlet, and how long an extension cord will be needed?

13. Are the instruments that will be needed available and in good tune and repair?

14. If the engagement is in a shopping center or similar setting, is there piped-in music? If so, can it be turned off? Who will be there to turn it off?

15. What other distractions are possibly going to be encountered? Is the group going to be trying to perform a concert of carols while Santa is arriving by helicopter just outside?

16. What will be the group's position in the facility? Will the choir be in two sections, whereas its members are used to being together? Will the choir be placed next to a gorgeous but noisely cascading waterfall or behind a beautifully lit fountain that is gurgling away?

17. Was the program originally planned with all kinds of marvelous lighting effects, whereas for some reason or other the lights cannot be turned off in the place where the performance will be held?

18. What will the engagement cost? Is it worth the cost for the results expected?

I am sure that many other interesting little problems could be added to this list by persons who have run into unexpected difficulties while trying to minister in a situation other than that which they were normally used to. I do not mean to discourage anyone from going out into the world to tell people about the saving love of Jesus Christ; what I am saying is that people should be prepared, that they should plan ahead, and that they should try to find out exactly what the group will be doing, where, when, how, with whom, and at what time.

Guest Musicians in The Church

What if the situation is reversed? What should be a church's policy about bringing in outside musicians? More specifically, should a church bring in outside musicians to train its musicians; and should a church bring outside musicians in as guest artists? The answer is yes in both cases. Using outside musicians is both acceptable and desirable if certain cautions are observed concerning persons being considered.

1. They must be better than anyone else in the church; otherwise a church is further ahead if it uses its own people. They cost nothing and likely will do nothing that is contrary to the expectations or doctrinal position of the church.
2. Their view of Scripture must parallel that of the host church or else their musical ideas will be colored by whatever their system of doctrine dictates, not by the host church's doctrine.
3. There must be sufficient benefit anticipated to offset the expense. It may be nice to think of flying in a Wyrtzen, Peterson, or Shea to chat with the choir, but it will not likely be a wise investment.
4. Furthermore, there must be sufficient interest and anticipated results to warrant hosting such a workshop (or whatever), considering the work involved.

It must be remembered that some things can be done with little or no money. Conductors from choirs of sister churches can be brought in, even if they are not as good as (or if they are better than!) the church's own conductor, just so the choir has the experience of sitting under different direction from time to time. The favor could be repaid in kind to the other churches. Also, when the host church's director is gone, his assistant could direct, giving him added exposure and practice. Moreover, the entire group could get permission to sit in (as spectators only) on a rehearsal of the local symphony chorus. In that way, the group is shown a different conducting technique and given the opportunity to hear a good quality group do some different styles of music.

A policy on bringing in guest artists will also depend on the position of the church and the minister of music. This policy will to some degree reflect two major attitudes: exclusion of outsiders, for one reason or another, and openness to using outsiders, for one reason or another. There are several reasons for each of those attitudes. Some of the reasons are good; some are not so good. If the church is closed to outside musicians because it is "better" than other churches, well, maybe it is, but I doubt it. If, on the other hand, the church is closed to outsiders in an effort to develop and use its own talent, that is quite a different thing. In either case, though, a closed church may lose out on some enriching experiences. On the other hand, a church may bring in every big name who is going through town in an effort to be *the* place where all the good things happen. But there are problems with that kind of attitude. If the church is open to quality musicians it thinks will have a ministry to its members as a whole, the church is likely to be enriched because of the experiences.

The thinking that holds true for bringing in guest artists who will perform for the whole church also holds true for bringing in guest experts to deal directly with the musical groups of the church. In everything that they do and stand for, they must enhance the total ministry of the local church. The attitude of the guest artist and guest expert and the attitude of the sponsoring church must both be above reproach and aimed at honoring God, building up His people, and bringing others to a saving knowledge of the Lord and Savior, Jesus Christ.

8

Music and Christian Education

This chapter deals with two aspects of the music that is a part of the Christian education program of the church: teaching music skills and teaching via music. We shall first consider the teaching of music skills as part of the offerings of the Sunday school or other related programs, and we shall then look at the use of these trained people in the ministry of teaching through music. Both ministries are important; neither of them should exist alone, and neither of them should be omitted from the courses considered by any Christian education department in any church that has the personnel necessary to teach such courses profitably and implement the use of people in teaching situations.

Music Classes

Many of the values of music must be taught to be appreciated—one example is the basic attitude of "creating" music each time it is played, as opposed to the idea that music is something that has been written down by someone, somewhere, and that the performer's only task is to put into sound what has already been written down. Music is more than ink and paper; it is something that can live, inspire, and speak to people who are desperately searching for something in life—something that has meaning, something that has beauty. Such values and attitudes are best passed along by people who have already learned them firsthand for themselves. In order for these things to be communicated to the bulk of the people in any church, therefore, it is expedient that there be as many "communicators" as possible. A formal training situation is the most efficient and personal way for this communication to take place. Various classes in music education could be offered, depending on the church's needs, resources, and aims of its music ministry. Some of these courses would be easily done as a class, while others are best handled individually. Classes could be offered in song leading, basic accompaniment skills, basic conducting, group voice lessons, basic theory, historical survey of church music, or even doctrinal survey courses for persons involved in the selection of choir anthems and hymns. The more advanced instruction offered in organ, piano, conducting, and so on is better served by individual lessons, but such instruction should not allow the trainee to work in isolation without using his skills in public. In the event that the particular church does not have competent teachers in these fields but feels that it needs someone trained in the area, outside help should be sought. The instructor could then be brought in or the individual students could go out to receive training; but the church should consider assuming the cost of this training.

Music workshops sponsored by various bodies are often held in the major centers around the country. They are usually very well done and are of lasting value to those who are able to participate in them. Usually there are intensive study sessions in many varied fields, and the person who attends gets much more in the way of practical, quality training in a short time than may be offered in any other form of training situation. It is well worth the church's money to send its music leaders to any of the workshops held in the church's area. I would suggest that these sessions are of real value not just for the minister of music but for all those who are in positions of leadership in the church music program, whether formally, as directors, pianists, or organists, or informally, as other influential persons in the program.

Two parts of the music program that contribute in a significant way to its growth and future stability are a fully developed, quality graded choir program and the ability to discover and then develop the talented individuals, of whatever age, who become part of that program. The matter of dealing with the various choirs is addressed in chapter four; and the importance of having a fully developed—"no holes"—program that is of high quality is obvious, for it supplies trained singers for the future ministry of the church. I have not so far discussed the other matter (discovering and then developing the talented individuals who emerge from the various age groups). Many churches have been blessed of God in a wonderful way with one or two superb accompanists, often persons who have been there for years. If those persons are both capable and willing to teach others their prized skills, the church is doubly fortunate, and, unfortunately, rare. A Christian's responsibility for converts does not end with bringing them to Christ. He must also make them disciples. His desire should be that they become like Christ. Surely such results come through those people's deep and intelligent study of the Scriptures, but they also come through Christians who pass on their skills in every area of ministry that is for the equipping of the saints for the work of the ministry. Stewardship is not limited to money, and discipleship is not limited to Bible study. Not all Christians are willing to be good stewards, and not all are willing to be discipled; but Christians who have skills and insights have the responsibility of teaching them to others who are willing to learn.

Using New Musicians

Those who are being taught can be used in a number of ways, depending on their abilities and the attitude of the particular church. A beginning organist should not play the organ on the Easter Sunday morning when the church is televising its service on a national network; but he could play for the midweek service, which is primarily attended by the core members of the church, who, it is hoped, not only will be sympathetic but also will be encouraged to see new talent being developed. Older youngsters who are training as accompanists could accompany the opening Sunday School sessions for the younger classes, if the church has opening sessions. Playing for opening sessions gives the older youngster exposure to the trials of playing for a group, and it will also very likely be encouraging, because the younger children will be thrilled to have "one of the big kids" playing for them—he will be an instant hero! There are drawbacks, though. The youth will be obliged to miss at least part of his own class time, and his absence may not be appreciated by him, his teacher, his parents, or perhaps all of them, and with some justification. The difficulty comes when an attempt is made to find a time when the young players can be used without introducing a conflict of scheduling. Some imagination and some cooperation are both required in ironing the matter out. Young men of upper high school age could play at a local mission or for the youth club meeting. If there is a group of people his age who want to sing, he may be selected to accompany them. It is recommended that young ladies who are learning be limited to the latter two options. Their skills may fit well a children's choir; they can be used for special numbers at youth club meetings or at some services; and so forth.

A word regarding *when* young players should be used: not before they are ready, and not long after. If they are not of a high enough caliber for the situation, they should not be used. The listeners will be frustrated or uncomfortable; the player himself will feel inadequate and ill prepared, and he may not wish to try it again very soon. On the other hand, if a young performer has the desire and the ability to do well in a public performance but is not given the opportunity to do so, he may lose interest in the music program of the church, the church itself, or in any participation in the church. He may be invited elsewhere to play and choose to leave his present church, largely because he was not given the opportunity to serve with the gifts, talents, and abilities that the Lord entrusted to him. Deciding on the right time to break in a young player is not an easy task. An audition, if having auditions is the policy established for everyone to be used in the ministry of music in the church, will soon reveal both his level of skill and his stage manner. If he is excessively nervous playing before the music committee or the minister of music, he will likely be worse when called on to play before the entire congregation. Obviously he is going to be apprehensive, anyone would be, but that is not what I mean by "excessively nervous." I mean that unusual situation in which a player capable of superior performance becomes somewhat impaired by the presence of others, resulting in an unusually inferior job.

Teaching Through Music

Now that some laymen have been trained in the basics of the various fields of music that were covered in the music classes in a Sunday school, they should be used as leaders. If one of them is leading hymns, it is hoped that he has been taught to use foundational, didactic hymns in Sunday school more than the favorite gospel songs or choruses, which are usually less solid theologically and often absolutely indefensible theologically. If one is singing a solo, it is hoped that he has learned that a disciplined and clear voice is desirable for singers of all ages so that the listeners can hear his clear words and understand his appropriate presentation. If one is a director, it is presumed that he too has learned that the music he conducts for Sunday must permeate the entirety of a Christian's life, and that there is value in teaching new songs to communicate new biblical truths which are not found in some of the more well known songs or which may be inadequately expressed there. Sunday school and club choirs, small groups of individuals who have a church sponsored outreach ministry, youth teams who work at the church camp during the summer, and the like could also be used to teach through music. In addition, music could be used to teach in every class. People sometimes understand scriptural truths better when they are presented in song than when they are taught in lectures.

Anything that conveys appropriately the messages of God as given in the Bible is a valuable addition to the Christian education emphasis of the local body of believers. All of the many facets of ministry which must be a part of any moving church have to be coordinated with one another and work together. Music is not just something that is performed by the choir and the soloist on Sunday morning; it is a way of expressing the Word of God. It should work in the teaching ministry of the church, in the discipleship ministry, in evangelism, and in the most important of all of the activities of the church, worship.

9

Music and Worship

Worship

Of the three basic functions of any ministry—worship, discipleship, and evangelism—worship is the most important. The reason is simple: a proper view of God will yield the other two aspects of the Christian life as a natural fruit of an adequate knowledge and appreciation of who God is and what He has done. Before any of the more mechanical points of worship can be examined, therefore, it is necessary for one to come to grips with his own view of God. Both the character of God and the nature of God are revealed in His attributes, as outlined in Scripture. This pushes back the question one step further and demands a settled position on the inspiration, inerrancy, efficaciousness, and infallibility of God's revelation of Himself as given in the Scriptures. Any wavering here will produce a wavering attitude toward the purpose of the worship service and therefore toward the execution of it. The place for one to begin, then, is with God and His Word. From there he is able to decide what his response to such a being will be, and that response will determine the meaning and content of the attitude and act of worship. A view of God and His Word that is anemic or is open to individual choice as to what is inspired and what is not will result in a life-style and a worship style that reflect those views. By contrast, a glimpse of the glory and majesty and holiness of God, as seen by Isaiah, can only yield the opposite response. Consider the words of Isaiah 6:1-8, presented here in the familiar yet magnificent King James Version:

> In the year that king Uzziah died I saw also the Lord sitting upon a throne, high and lifted up, and his train filled the temple.
>
> Above it stood the seraphims: each one had six wings; with twain he covered his face, and with twain he covered his feet, and with twain he did fly.
>
> And one cried unto another, and said, Holy, holy, holy, is the LORD of hosts: the whole earth is full of his glory.
>
> And the posts of the door moved at the voice of him that cried, and the house was filled with smoke.
>
> Then said I, Woe is me! for I am undone; because I am a man of unclean lips, and I dwell in the midst of a people of unclean lips: for mine eyes have seen the King, the LORD of hosts.
>
> Then flew one of the seraphims unto me, having a live coal in his hand, which he had taken with the tongs from off the altar:
>
> And he laid it upon my mouth, and said, Lo, this hath touched thy lips; and thine iniquity is taken away, and thy sin purged.
>
> Also I heard the voice of the Lord, saying, Whom shall I send, and who will go for us? Then said I, Here am I; send me.

This passage, perhaps more than any other, is an example of worship on its highest plane. It begins with a vision of the transcendent God. Notice the descriptions "sitting upon a throne, high and lifted up, and his train filled the temple. . . . Holy, holy, holy . . . : the whole earth is full of his glory. . . . And the house was filled with smoke." Those words describe a person who is totally beyond anything human. They speak both of the majesty of God and of His mystery; He is the Holy Other.

Isaiah's immediate reaction comes from a proper view of himself, and he immediately confesses that he is a sinner in need of cleansing. The King, the Lord of hosts, likewise responds instantly by providing immediate and total cleansing. After those three actions have taken place, then, and only then, does God call for a response from the worshiper. Only after the vision of God, the recognition of one's own sin, and the purification that God alone can provide, is a person called to serve Him.

There is another order to be observed here. There is the proclamation of God's character in the seraph cries of "Holy, holy, holy"; then there is the dialogue between God (through His spokesman) and His people—a dialogue that is a result of the spokesman's having received of God's grace himself and then giving back to God his service of love by the proclamation of His message. Leaders in the church should observe this order and see that others observe it. Leaders do not speak for themselves; they do not minister of themselves (1 Peter 4:11). Rather, it is for God that they speak: it is God whom they serve. They are called to be servants of God, but to be leaders of His people. As they lead, they should lead with a sensitivity to the heart of God and to the needs of the people. It is often better for leaders to lead people by the hand than to be so far ahead of them that they can hardly see where their leaders are, let alone where they are going; and it is worse yet when people try following such leaders.

Leading in worship means just that, then. Leaders are to be worshipers themselves, and they are to direct everyone present to the proper view of God, which will yield the correct response of attitude to Him. The pastors, choirs, and soloists—the leaders—are not to be the only ones worshiping almost on behalf of the rest, but everyone present is to be led to Christ by what the leaders say and do. Worship is not a spectator sport; it demands participation. And the participation should be wholehearted, sincere, and based on the truth of God's Word. It should involve the total person, beginning with his mind, then his will in deciding to honor the Lord in his heart, and then his emotions as his person is totally overwhelmed by the nature of God. Worship is not only activity; first it is an attitude toward God and His revelation of Himself. This will undoubtedly result in some form of activity; and so it should, as it did in the case of Isaiah. But mere activity is not the primary goal to be sought. Lovelace and Rice put it this way: "Worship, however, is more than action and interaction between God and man, it must be *worthy* action. Worthship, the original meaning of the word, suggests that our worship be worthy of the God whom we praise."[1]

The Mechanics of Worship

Thus we come to a consideration of the mechanics of the worship service: How are we going to worship God in a worthy manner? I begin with a word of explanation about the term *mechanics*, which I use to describe the things done in the worship service. It is intended to refer simply to the technical aspects of the time spent and is not in any way intended to convey the idea that the things done should be done in a mechanical way. I hope that the remainder of this chapter will indicate what I mean by *mechanics*; but I offer this word of explanation here to alleviate fears that I advocate a routine that is ideal and is to be adhered to, for that is not the case.

Worship should inspire, sustain, encourage, motivate, strengthen, and support the worshiper. Each activity of the worship service should create attitudes of consistency (for God is immutable), alertness (for one should not want to miss a moment of being in His presence), yet relaxation in an atmosphere of contemplation so that each individual may hear God speaking to him without interruption from those around. All those attitudes require the expenditure of energy: mental energy, for concentrating on the message of the songs and for praying; and physical energy, for singing, praising, or simply sitting still in respect of others around who may be disturbed

---

[1]Austin C. Lovelace and William C. Rice, *Music and Worship in the Church* (Nashville: Abingdon, 1976), p. 23.

by activity and thus be unable to worship. Everyone must be given the opportunity to worship God. When it is time to sing a hymn, it does not matter if some people do not have great voices; what does matter is whether or not people have a song. As with all things, singing that lacks sincerity, justice, righteousness, and honesty before God is an abomination in His sight (Psalm 51; Hosea 6:6; Amos 5:18-27). God is concerned with the inner man, not with the outward formality; He is concerned with the genuineness of worship, not with the structure of it; He is concerned about the degree of real quality, not about the relative quality: God does not take a person's individual worship and compare it with that of another person; He measures each person's worship against the attitudes of the person's heart. If a person's worship could be better but he does not give it the effort that would make it better, I fear that it will not be as pleasing to God as He would like it to be. He has loved with an everlasting and total love; and He must often be disappointed at people's dismal attempts to thank Him for it, for all too often they are so busy running programs or asking for things for themselves that they neglect entirely to recognize the person of God and His work not only for themselves but also for the entire world. Thus they forget to thank Him.

There should be a striving for excellence in all that a person does for God, which in point of fact is all that a person does. Yet this striving for excellence must not lead to pride, arrogance, or even the tacet worship of the form rather than the God of all creation. Donald Hustad has pointed this out by saying (in an informal lecture) that "music is a cultural language, and what is 'fittin' and 'proper' in one culture is not acceptable in another. Music makes sense *only* in the culture for which it was intended." King David said the following upon the occasion of the purchase of the threshing floor of Iranah: "I will not offer burnt offerings to the LORD my God which cost me nothing" (2 Sam. 24:24, NASB). To do well *is* to praise. To preach, help, sing, study, enjoy creation, or enjoy creating—anything that is done well—is to do something to His honor. Surely the public worship service ought to be so excellent that it becomes a window that the world can look through and see God.

A Presbyterian church in Greenville, South Carolina, once chose this epigram and made it public, expressing the desire for it not to be true of the church's number, as it is of so many people: "Too many Christians worship their work, work at their play, and play at their worship." God help Christians if that is the norm. They are gathered together to hear from God and to talk to Him—they should sit up and pay attention.

The worship service is a corporate experience, and as such its music should speak to everyone, as much as is possible. The service should lead all the people into an attitude of worship; into the work of building up and feeding each other from the resources of God; and into the work of pointing each other to Him, to His purpose for lives, and to His control of all of history. Christians ought to point to Him in all things, and never to themselves or to the activities in which they are engaged. He is the all-important one. Programs are not to supplant Him under any circumstances, and yet they are some primary tools in reaching people for God and in reaching God as a people. The problem is coming to that middle ground of utility without straying off into formality that is without life. God is the creator of all things, and He has granted to man, in His image, the right and ability to create as well. It is expedient for His worship that Christians *be* creative in their thinking and in the execution of the worship service.

Guidelines for Music in Worship

Music is invaluable as a worship tool for this reason: it is something that needs to be re-created at each performance. Each time an anthem is sung or a hymn is used, it must come as a fresh, new, and vital part of the worship time. Music has the power to enhance and reinforce the spoken parts of the service. It can speak on its own, too. A great organ prelude or a great choral anthem *is* praise to God, it *is* part of worship, and very often it is also the best possible means of expression when mere words seem inadequate. When it comes to knowing just which music will best serve the purpose in a given situation, God should be asked in faith and He will supply wisdom (James 1:5-6). Other concrete factors can be used as guidelines in making this decision, including the following:

1. Music should not be used to manipulate; it should be used to guide and encourage, but not to cajole or manipulate.
2. All the activities of the service should mesh to provide as complete an opportunity for worship as is possible. The ultimate purpose of creation is to glorify God, and any other functions should be in line with that purpose. There will be a variety of worshipers, who will come with a variety of needs. The service should include opportunities for all four of the aspects of worship given in Isaiah 6:1-8 (see pages 137-39), in order to provide for the participation of everyone in the adoration of God.
3. God is alive, and His mercies are new every morning—yet the same old hymns are sung in the same old way with the same old attitudes. The laziness of sameness and routine should be avoided. The character of God should be allowed to inspire a little variety. A little thought should be put into the service—not just the what, but also the who, the how, and the why. If just one of those elements is not as it should be, it may discolor all the rest.
4. When variety in music is considered (as mentioned in number three above), it should be remembered that there is value both in well-known music and in new or unknown music. Music that is dear to someone's heart will cause him to recall precious times with the Lord and His people and will lead him again to praise God. On the other hand, music

that is unknown can lead to praise by its very character. People know that they should march when a march is played, and they relax when a lullaby is sung, and, in much the same manner, most Christians know how to worship when a song of praise or adoration is sung. The difficulty comes when proper attitudes are not present; then people do not worship; instead, their minds wander and they lose precious moments in God's presence.

5. Another point related to variety in music (see points three and four above) is that of using "reruns." Example: The service is begun with the teaching of a new hymn, the choir sings a related anthem, and then the congregation breaks into a magnificent time of spontaneous praise and telling of needs. What a memorable evening! Six months later the same hymn and choir anthem are scheduled, but nothing happens. Why? God has moved on, the people have moved on, and anything repeated is not "playing to the same house" and so will not be similarly received.

6. Only those performing musicians who are living exemplary lives should be used. People who perform public ministries should meet the same qualifications as those of other church leaders, as a general rule. Ministry in music should be just that, with the ministry coming first and the music as the medium of expression. Someone should not be expected to lead in something he is not fully able to do himself.

7. The content of every song used should fit a proper theology. Martin Luther is credited as having said this:

> I have no use for cranks who despise music, because it is a gift of God. . . . Next after theology I give to music the highest place and the greatest honor. . . . Next to the Word of God only music deserves to be extolled as mistress and governess of the feelings of the human heart.

Luther indeed recognized the importance of music, but more important here is the fact that he made it secondary to the truth of the Word.

8. Being prolific does not make a composer good. Some composers and arrangers manage to maintain a better average than others, but no one writes consistently good material. The father of British hymnody, Charles Wesley, is credited with writing 7,270 hymns, but even his were not all good. Authors and composers who seem to put out good work quite regularly should be found and their material used, but their every work should not be expected to be great.
9. Music for the various groups should be selected according to the members' ages, needs, and so forth, as outlined in chapter five.
10. As a further check on the suitability of the songs selected, all the participants in the particular service could get together to go over every detail of the service ahead of time. (This would, of course, have to be done at least a week ahead of time to allow for any changes.) This meeting will have the added benefit of getting all the persons involved thinking in the same groove, which should heighten their awareness of the service and produce a spirit of unity of purpose and emphasis, which can only help.

With these guiding principles in mind, more nitty-gritty decisions can be made. How many hymns, and what kinds of hymns, should be used? How many songs, and what kinds of songs, is the choir to do? What should the order of service be? Should a printed order of service be used? How many special numbers should be included, and what kinds of numbers should they be—group numbers, solos, instrumental numbers? More basic yet is the question of who makes these decisions. And what about the choice of music used by the soloists and others who are "independent" of the organizational structure of the church? And what happens if a soloist needs training, helpful suggestions, advice, or criticism? Where does "the buck" stop? Certainly many of the answers to these questions will differ from congregation to congregation, but guidelines for some of them can be stated.

The basic question of who makes the decisions is a good place to start, since answers to the other questions depend largely on the answer to this one. If there is a minister of music, he is ultimately responsible for the entire music department. Thus any advice, suggestions to groups or individuals, or criticism falls within his area of responsibility, with one possible exception. If there is a possibility that hard feelings may result, the minister of music may wish to meet with the music committee to get its opinion and support. The minister of music may then approach the person concerned on behalf of the music committee. The advantage of this procedure is that if the person to be approached is prone to getting upset, it will be less damaging to the total ministry of the church if he is upset with a changing administrative group than with any individual. There are two exceptions to this exception, however! One is if the person to be approached is the chairman of the music committee, and the other is if a very serious problem develops out of the situation. The minister of music must be willing, in love and by virtue of his position, to lay his own neck on the line rather than to implicate a whole group in a nasty situation. He is the chief executive officer of the music program and must assume responsibility for it. Should he need further assistance, he should turn to the senior minister, who may be in a position to help him further.

The number and kinds of hymns and songs to be used is the decision of the leadership of the church. I would like to make one suggestion about the ministry of the senior choir, though. In addition to any service music—a call to worship, prayer responses, a benediction—it is good if the choir can do two selections on a Sunday morning: an anthem that is objective in scope, is based on a scriptural quotation or theme, and is basically Godward in emphasis; and a hymn arrangement or gospel song that, by contrast, is more subjective in nature and more peopleward in emphasis. Variety in the tempos, styles, and volumes of the two numbers should be aimed at. Thus everyone should have something to his liking and find something that ministers to him. Again the point is well made that the best music possible should be used, but it should be remembered that Bach is not better if neither the congregation nor the choir can handle it.

What then should be the order of service? What about the use of a printed program? The order of service is to be the servant of those leading the service. It is not law. If a printed program is used, and I believe it should be used, it should be general enough to give some flexibility in the serivce, should flexibility be desired. An item that simply reads "Closing Hymn" is much more open to fitting the path the message takes than if a specific hymn is selected ahead of time, unless the senior minister, or whoever is preaching that service, knows for sure in advance what his concluding comments and main point of emphasis will be. On the other hand, if a detailed program is issued to the congregation, everything should not be announced. If the bulletin says that hymn thirty-five is to come next, the introduction should be played and the singing started. Anything else does one of two things: it either assumes ignorance in the congregation or it makes it appear that the contents of the written program, including all the announcements of coming activities, are not really all that important, otherwise the important ones would not be announced orally. Just as a sidelight here, oral announcements that do not apply to everyone should not be made, for the service is a corporate activity. If a printed order of service is not used, or if a fairly general order is used, a claim to spontaneity should not actually be a cover for being too lazy to pick the hymns in time to get them into the bulletin!

The feeling of spontaneity often comes only as the result of many hours of planning and work. A naturally flowing service takes planning and preparation on the part of all who will participate. Variety comes via a similar route. If the leaders in the church think that variety could be used to advantage, they should obtain training in some different methods of presenting the truths of God's Word. There are books, people, and classes that can supply information on many different forms of communication. Concerts are obvious, but what about using a dialogue between two of the pastors, or the pastor and a layman? A monologue, in the form of simple pulpit drama, could bring to life a Scripture reading that the people have heard many times before but never seen in such a fresh light. There is no written law that the choir must sit in the choir loft and wear robes; maybe they could just sit as part of the congregation ready to sing a communion song just before the elements are served, or maybe they could begin the service by quietly beginning to sing "Brethren, We Have Met to Worship" or a similar piece. These, as most ideas for variety, take a bit of knowledge, a bit of imagination, but mostly time in looking for ideas and then thinking them through.

Part of a varied service could include teaching the congregation a new hymn. This is often a tense time for both the song leader and the congregation. All too often he ends up singing a virtual solo while the people who are supposed to be worshiping are standing there gritting their teeth, hating every minute of it. That need not be the case. If the organist would include a simple arrangement of the piece in his prelude, the tune would already be somewhat familiar to the congregation, though subconsciously. If the choir director would take ten minutes out of his choir rehearsal to teach the hymn to the choir, about seven or eight percent of the congregation (the usual number of people in the choir) would thoroughly know the piece, and that would help the congregation unbelievably as well as establish the tempo for the accompanists. Then, just before the congregation is to sing the new hymn, the song leader could read the text as poetry while the organist quietly plays through the score once again. In that way, both the text and the tune would be familiar to a certain extent, adding greatly to the reception of the new hymn. Any background information could also be given, but technical musical explanations should be avoided; they will be neither understood nor appreciated.

If the theme or purpose of the service is out of the ordinary, variety is not hard to find. A funeral will use some different music from that likely to be used at a wedding, though both should include praise if the person or persons involved are Christians. Missions conferences, evangelistic crusades, youth or children's meetings, and services of ordination or dedication will all have their unique emphases and will in themselves be sources of musical variety in the church. If the almost endless number of pieces of music available for use by the musicians in the church is added to that, there need not be any more unthought, routine, or dull music in the service of Christ.

A point brought out earlier in this book was the important item regarding evaluation of the program. Evaluation should be part of the review of each service. Again, if nothing is aimed at, it is sure that nothing will be hit. Definite goals for each service should be set, and afterwards the service should be evaluated to see how it measured up to those goals. What needs to be preserved? What went well, and why? What could be profitably added? What should be modified? What should be done away with entirely? As stewards of the resources of Christ and of His church, Christians had better be sure that there is both reason for and value in everything they do. Now, it stands to reason that a person cannot measure the growth of each individual in the service, and a person may not even know right away of decisions made for Christ, but a person can evaluate even the intangible factors for determining the value of a given service. Subjective feelings about a service are often good indicators, and comments from the other church leaders and the people at large should also be considered in the evaluation process. But any program must rely on God, who is the purpose, end, sustainer, and source of power for all the activities of all the participants, in order for the program really to be a success.

The world around is looking at Christians to see if they—and their God—are for real. The saints of all the ages are watching to see how the work they have begun is being carried on. The angels are gazing in amazement at how people treat the name of Jesus. God Himself is alert to every deed, plan, thought, and attitude so that He might accurately reward or discipline. And Jesus is tenderly looking to Christians to finish His work, not because salvation is incomplete, but because the roll of heaven is.

"There are souls to rescue, there are souls to save,
Send the light!
Send the light!"

Charles H. Gabriel

Moody Press, a ministry of the Moody Bible Institute, is designed for education, evangelization and edification. If we may assist you in knowing more about Christ and the Christian life, please write us without obligation to:
Moody Press, c/o MLM, Chicago, Illinois 60610.

Bibliography

There are many ways in which these resources could be listed, but I have chosen to group them under the general categories of Church Music, Conducting, Music Groups, Theory and History, Applied Music, Other Helpful Books, Periodicals, and Articles. Although each of these resources deals with more than one category, they are all classified according to the primary topic to which they refer. Many of the resources express views others than evangelical but are of value for their general information.

The best book on music in the church is probably Lovelace and Rice's *Music and Worship in the Church*, and the best book on the ministry of the church is probably Ortlund's *Up with Worship*.

Church Music

Ashton, Joseph N. *Music in Worship*. Boston: Pilgrim, 1943.

Bonner, Clint. *A Hymn Is Born*. Nashville: Broadman, 1959.

Campbell, Sidney S. *Music in the Church*. London: Dennis Dobson, 1951.

Cleall, Charles. *Music and Holiness*. London: Epworth, 1964.

Davidson, Archibald T. *Church Music*. Cambridge: Harvard U. Press, 1960.

DeVinney, Richard. *There's More to Church Music Than Meets the Ear*. Philadelphia: Fortress, 1972.

Halter, Carl. *The Practice of Sacred Music*. St. Louis: Concordia, 1955.

Kerr, Phil. *Music in Evangelism*. 4th ed. Glendale, Calif.: Gospel Music Publishers, 1954.

Larson, Bob. *Hippies, Hindus, and Rock and Roll*. McCook, Nebr.: Bob Larson, 1969.

———. *Rock and Roll: The Devil's Diversion*. McCook, Nebr.: Bob Larson, 1970.

———. *Rock and the Church*. Carol Stream, Ill.: Creation House, 1971.

Lovelace, Austin C., and Rice, William C. *Music and Worship in the Church*. Nashville: Abingdon, 1976.

Ortlund, Anne. *Up with Worship*. Glendale, Calif.: Regal, 1975.

Osbeck, Kenneth W. *The Ministry of Music*. Grand Rapids: Zondervan, 1961.

Steere, Dwight. *Music in Protestant Worship*. Richmond, Va.: John Knox, 1960.

Thayer, Lynn W. *The Church Music Handbook*. Grand Rapids: Zondervan, 1971.

Thomas, Edith Lovell. *Music in Christian Education*. New York: Abingdon, 1953.

Topp, Dale. *Music in the Christian Community*. Grand Rapids: Eerdmans, 1977.

Tovey, Herbert G. *Music Levels in Christian Education*. Wheaton: Van Kempen, 1952.

Urang, Gunnar. *Church Music for the Glory of God*. Moline, Ill.: Christian Service Foundation, 1956.

Conducting

Bostock, Donald. *Choirmastery*. Aylesbury, England: Epworth, 1966.

Decker, Harold A., and Herford, Julius, eds. *Choral Conducting: A Symposium*. New York: Appleton-Century-Crofts, 1973.

Ehmann, Wilhelm. *Choral Directing*. Minneapolis: Augsburg, 1968.

Garretson, Robert L. *Conducting Choral Music*. Boston: Allyn and Bacon, 1970.

Hoffelt, Robert O. *How to Lead Informal Singing*. Nashville: Abingdon, 1961.

Lamb, Gordon H. *Choral Techniques*. Dubuque, Iowa: William C. Brown, 1974.

Rudolf, Max. *The Grammar of Conducting*. New York: Schirmer, 1950.

Thomas, Kurt. *The Choral Conductor*. New York: Associated Music Publishers, 1971.

MUSIC GROUPS

Jacobs, Ruth Krehbiel. *The Children's Choir*. Philadelphia: Fortress, 1958.

Mees, Arthur. *Choirs and Choral Music*. New York: Haskell House, 1901.

Sydnor, James R. *The Training of Church Choirs*. Nashville: Abingdon, 1963.

Trobian, Helen. *The Instrumental Ensemble in the Church*. Nashville: Abingdon, 1963.

THEORY AND HISTORY

Appleby, David P. *History of Church Music*. Chicago: Moody, 1965.

Douglas, Winfred. *Church Music in History and Practice*. New York: Scribner's, 1962.

Foote, Henry Wilder. *Three Centuries of American Hymnody*. Archon Books, 1968.

Jacobs, Arthur. *Choral Music*. Baltimore: Penguin, 1963.

Leimohn, Edwin. *The Singing Church*. Columbus: Wartburg, 1959.

Squire, Russel N. *Church Music*. St. Louis: Bethany Press, 1962.

Warburton, Annie O. *Melody Writing and Analysis*. London: Longman, 1960.

APPLIED MUSIC

Andreas, and Fowells. *The Voice of Singing*. New York: Carl Fischer, 1970.

Ingram, Madeline, and Rice, William C. *Vocal Technique for Children and Youth*. Nashville: Abingdon, 1962.

Klotz, Hans. *The Organ Handbook*. St. Louis: Concordia, 1969.

Marshall, Madeleine. *The Singer's Manual of English Diction*. New York: Schirmer, 1953.

Mathis, William S. *The Pianist and Church Music*. Nashville: Abingdon, 1962.

Rice, William C. *Basic Principles of Singing*. Nashville: Abingdon, 1961.

Walter, Samuel. *Basic Principles of Service Playing*. Nashville: Abingdon, 1963.

Other Helpful Books

Carnegie, Dale. *How to Win Friends and Influence People*. New York: Pocket Books, 1936, 1964.

Dobson, James. *Dare to Discipline*. Wheaton: Tyndale, 1970.

The International Center for Learning. *Ways to Help Them Learn* (G/L Publications: Glendale, Calif.). A series of books that give age-level characteristics for preschoolers through adults.

PERIODICALS

Choral Praise, Music Makers, Opus 1, Opus 2, The Church Musican, The Music Leader. Sunday School Board of the Southern Baptist Convention (127 Ninth Avenue, North, Nashville, Tenn. 37234).

Letters. The Chorister's Guild (P.O. Box 38188, Dallas, Tex. 75238).

ARTICLES

Best, Harold. "Music: Offerings of Creativity." *Christianity Today*, May 6, 1977.

Bilhorn, Clem. "How to Gain Permission for Use of Copyrighted Songs." Baptist General Conference reprint.

———. "Trends in Contemporary Church Music." Baptist General Conference reprint.

Blanc, Ronald. "Institute of Church Imperatives." First Baptist Church of Modesto, Calif.

Cook, Robert. "A Mini Course in Copyright." *Moody Monthly*, April 1977.

———. "That New Religious Music." *Moody Monthly*, April 1977.

Hustad, Donald. "Music Speaks . . . But What Language?" *Christianity Today*, May 6, 1977.

"Leadership." *The Christian Link*, September 1974. Central Canada Baptist Conference.

"Mini-Course in Copyright." Shawnee Press; Delaware Water Gap.

Oliver, Kay. "You *Can* Be a Songleader." *Moody Monthly,* April 1977.

Pennington, James. "Rock Music—Love ad Infinitum ad Absurdum." *Christianity Today*, July 8, 1977.

"People Caring for People." Baptist General Conference reprint.

Schaller, Lyle. "What Is Your Frame of Reference?" Baptist General Conference reprint.

Index